MITTLERER SCHULABSCHLUSS

SEK I

Mündliche Prüfung Englisch

Brandenburg

STARK

S. 1: Joe Gough/Dreamstime.com
S. 3, 4, 6, 9, 11, 13, 14, 20, 35, 37, 59, 61, 77, 86: Paul Jenkinson
S. 28: Nick Winchester/www.sxc.hu
S. 38: Stan McMurtry, Daily Mail, 2nd September 2003
S. 40, 64: Stan McMurtry, Daily Mail, 10th June 2003
S. 42: From *The car that drives itself* by Ray Massey, Daily Mail, 31st August 2005
S. 71: James Moore

ISBN: 3-89449-818-8

D-85318 Freising · Postfach 1852 · Tel. (0 81 61) 1790

Inhalt

Fortsetzung siehe nächste Seite

Autoren:
Hinweise zur mündlichen Prüfung: Steffen Bunzeck
Training und Aufgaben im Stil der mündlichen Prüfung: Paul Jenkinson

Vorwort

Liebe Schülerin, lieber Schüler,

dieses Buch wendet sich an alle, die sich an Oberschulen, Gesamtschulen mit gymnasialer Oberstufe, Gymnasien und Förderschulen in Brandenburg auf die mündliche Prüfung am Ende der Klasse 10 vorbereiten.

Das Buch besteht aus einem Trainings- und einem Prüfungskapitel.

- Das Kapitel „**Training**" ist wiederum zweigeteilt.
  Im ersten Teil erfährst du, wie du deine **mündliche Sprachkompetenz** schrittweise **steigern** und **vervollkommnen** kannst. Außerdem lernst du hier Möglichkeiten kennen, Gespräche – z. B. auch dein Prüfungsgespräch – aktiv zu bestimmen. Lies diese Seiten genau durch. In den **Hinweiskästen** findest du neben **allgemeinen Regeln zur Gesprächsführung** viele **Redewendungen**, die du unbedingt auswendig lernen solltest.
  Im zweiten Teil dieses Kapitels kannst du den **Umgang mit** den **Materialien** üben, die dir als Ausgangsbasis für das Prüfungsgespräch vorgelegt werden. Auch hier helfen dir wieder die Tipps und Informationen in den Hinweiskästen.
  Zu beiden Bereichen des Trainingskapitels gibt es zahlreiche, nach Schwierigkeitsgrad geordnete **Trainingsaufgaben**, die du alleine, zum Teil aber auch zusammen mit deinen Klassenkameraden lösen kannst. Anschließend könnt ihr eure Lernfortschritte anhand der **Lösungsvorschläge** überprüfen.
- Das zweite Kapitel enthält eine Auswahl von **Materialien und Aufgaben**, wie sie dir im Rahmen deiner mündlichen Prüfung begegnen könnten. So kannst du deine Fähigkeiten quasi unter „Prüfungsbedingungen" erproben. Selbstverständlich sind auch die Aufgaben dieses Teils mit ausführlichen **Lösungsvorschlägen** versehen.

So vorbereitet meisterst du deine mündliche Prüfung sicherlich mit Bravur.
Viel Erfolg!

Hinweise zur mündlichen Prüfung

Für alle Schülerinnen und Schüler der Oberschulen, Gesamtschulen, Gymnasien und Förderschulen, die nach den Rahmenlehrplänen für die Sekundarstufe I unterrichtet werden, findet am Ende der Jahrgangsstufe 10 eine Prüfung statt.

Dabei legt jeder Schüler
- eine schriftliche Prüfung in Deutsch,
- eine schriftliche Prüfung in Mathematik,
- eine mündliche Prüfung in einer Fremdsprache und
- eine mündliche Prüfung in einem weiteren Pflicht- oder Wahlpflichtfach ab.

Die Schüler können mit Zustimmung ihrer Eltern wählen, ob sie in der ersten Fremdsprache oder in der zweiten, seit der 7. Jahrgangsstufe unterrichteten Fremdsprache geprüft werden möchten.

Vor der mündlichen Prüfung haben die Schüler auf Wunsch die Möglichkeit, prüfungsbezogene fachliche Fragen mit dem Prüfer zu besprechen. Prüfer ist in der Regel die Lehrkraft, die in der Jahrgangsstufe 10 die Fremdsprache unterrichtet hat.

Die mündlichen Prüfungen in der Fremdsprache sind in der Regel **Gruppenprüfungen mit bis zu vier Schülern**. Eine Gruppenprüfung dauert mindestens 25 und höchstens 50 Minuten. Die Gruppen werden vom unterrichtenden Lehrer eingeteilt; allerdings können die Schüler im Unterricht und insbesondere in der Vorbereitungsphase Wünsche für die Zusammenstellung ihrer Gruppe äußern.

Unmittelbar vor der Prüfung wird den Schülern unter Aufsicht eine Vorbereitungszeit eingeräumt. Der Zeitrahmen wird vom Prüfer festgelegt und beträgt zwischen 20 und 30 Minuten. Während der Vorbereitungszeit kann jeder Schüler Aufzeichnungen anfertigen. Diese werden dem Prüfer nach der Prüfung übergeben. Bei Gruppenaufgaben kann den Schülern die Gelegenheit gegeben werden, sich während der Vorbereitungszeit zu beraten. Über diese Möglichkeit entscheidet der Fachausschuss der jeweiligen Schule.

Das Prüfungsgespräch besteht aus mindestens 2 Teilen. Im ersten Teil erhält jeder Schüler eine Teilaufgabe, die er selbstständig zu bearbeiten und darzustellen hat. Im zweiten Teil findet ein Gespräch innerhalb der Gruppe statt, das sich schwerpunktmäßig auf die vorhergehenden Teilaufgaben beziehen soll.

Unmittelbar nach der mündlichen Prüfung berät der Fachausschuss über die Prüfungsleistungen. Aus dem Ergebnis der Prüfung und der Jahresnote wird eine Abschlussnote gebildet. Dabei geht die Jahresnote mit 60 % und das Ergebnis der Prüfung mit 40 % in die Abschlussnote ein. Das Ergebnis der Prüfung und die Abschlussnote werden dem Schüler im Anschluss an die Beratung bekannt gegeben.

Die Prüfungsaufgaben werden vom Prüfer erarbeitet. Sie beziehen sich auf die Themen und Teilthemen der Rahmenlehrpläne und kommen schwerpunktmäßig aus dem Unterricht der Jahrgangsstufen 9 und 10, wobei auch Kenntnisse, Fähigkeiten und Fertigkeiten aus den vorhergehenden Schuljahren verlangt werden. Die Aufgabenstellung wird den Schülern zu Beginn der Prüfung schriftlich vorgelegt. Es besteht keine Auswahlmöglichkeit unter mehreren Aufgaben.

Folgende Themen werden im Unterricht der Jahrgangsstufen 9 und 10 behandelt:
- Values and education
- Politics and economy
- Past – present – future
- The role of the media
- Diversity in a multicultural society
- Environment and health care

▶ Training

1 Sprechfertigkeiten verbessern

Sich in einer Fremdsprache mündlich auszudrücken, ist nicht einfach – schon gar nicht im Rahmen einer Prüfung oder sogar einer Gruppenprüfung. Man kann sich auch nicht kurzfristig – quasi über Nacht – auf diesen Prüfungsbereich vorbereiten. Wenn man in einer mündlichen Prüfung gut abschneiden will, muss man langfristig und nachhaltig an der Sprechfertigkeit arbeiten.
Übungsmöglichkeiten bietet dir der (tägliche) Englischunterricht. Nimm aktiv am Unterrichtsgeschehen teil, d. h. melde dich so oft wie möglich und sprich auf Englisch. So gewinnst du mit der Zeit Routine und wirst nach und nach gelassener. Wenn du dabei künftig auch noch die folgenden grundsätzlichen Tipps und Hinweise berücksichtigst, klappt das mit der Zeit sicherlich recht gut.

- Sprich deutlich und nicht zu schnell.
- Frage nach, wenn du etwas nicht verstanden hast.
- Vermeide einfache, kurze Antworten wie *yes / no*. Mit solchen Antworten kannst du keine Gespräche in Gang halten und auch deine mündlichen Fähigkeiten nicht unter Beweis stellen.
- Lerne, Sachverhalte auf unterschiedliche Weise auszudrücken, damit du nicht ständig dieselben Formulierungen wiederholst.
- Versuche die Unterhaltung selbst zu bestimmen, vor allem in Gruppendiskussionen. Auf diese Weise sprichst du über **deine** Themen, hast mehr zu sagen und bist selbstbewusster bei dem, was du sagst.

1. A *yes/no* reply does not make conversation. Expand your answers to the following questions as much as possible. Before speaking spend a few minutes thinking about what you can say.

a) Do you like sport?

b) Do you think fast food is bad for you?

c) Do you think it will be difficult for you to get a job when you leave school?

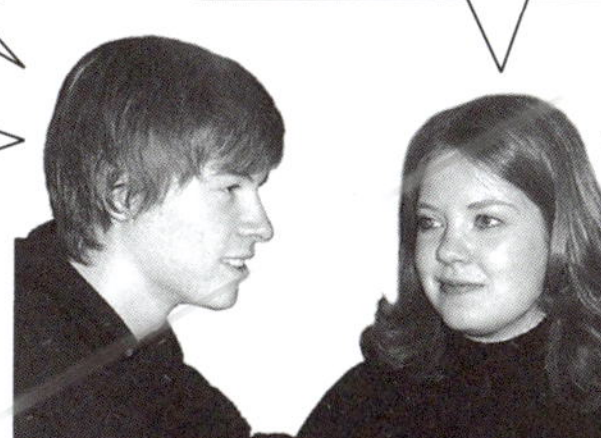

d) Would you like to visit another country on an exchange?

e) Have you ever thought of becoming a vegetarian?

2. You are given a short answer in brackets *(Klammern)* for each question. Make these answers more detailed and interesting by adding as much information as possible using complete sentences.

a) How do you get to school?
(*Answer*: by car)

b) Which newspaper do you like reading?
(*Answer: for example,* Märkische Allgemeine)

c) What is your favourite television programme?
(*Answer: for example*, Frontal 21)

d) If you could go to America, what would you particularly like to see?
(*Answer*: Manhattan)

e) What colour is the school uniform?
(*Answer*: black and green)

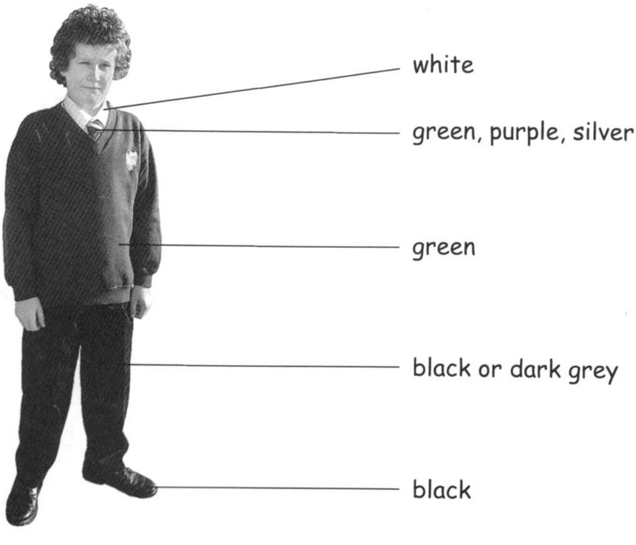

3. Synonyms: Use a different word with almost the same meaning for each of the underlined ones. Remember **you** are the person talking – this is not reported speech.

a) Possible synonyms for *think* are: ______________________________

"I think the British royal family is very interesting. I think that Prince Charles should become the next king. But I don't think many British people will like Camilla as their queen. If Charles doesn't become king, I think Prince William will then be the next one. I don't think that Britain will ever be without its royal family."

b) Possible synonyms for *then* when used in a sequence of events are:

____

"In the morning I wake up and then go to the bathroom. Then I have a wash and then I get dressed. Then I go downstairs and have my breakfast. Then I get my school things and then leave my house for school."

c) Possible synonyms for *told (told us)* are: ______________________________
Possible synonyms for *visit* are: ______________________________

"It was funny listening to my friend when he told us his story. He told us about his visit to England. His visit was a disaster. He told us how he missed the plane and then told us about how he got lost in London."

4. When talking you often need to think of a suitable synonym for something. How quickly can you think of suitable synonyms for the following list of words?

(to) shout ______________________________
house ______________________________
pupils ______________________________
(to) tell ______________________________
area ______________________________
tourists ______________________________
religion ______________________________
teenager ______________________________
the newspapers ______________________________
dirty ______________________________

5. Speaking clearly: Look at what someone says about their school.

a) Read the paragraph out loud, preferably into a tape recorder.

"My school is a typical English comprehensive in a small town with about 1400 pupils including the sixth-form students. Many of the school's pupils come from small villages in the area. These children have to be brought to school by bus."

b) Read the paragraph again with these differences: / is for a short pause, // is for a long pause and <u>underlined</u> words are spoken together as a group of words without any breaks.

"<u>My school</u> <u>is a typical</u> <u>English comprehensive</u> <u>in a small town</u> <u>with about 1400 pupils</u> / <u>including the sixth-form students</u>. // <u>Many of the school's pupils</u> <u>come from small villages in the area</u>. // <u>These children have to be brought to school</u> <u>by bus</u>."

c) Give spoken details about your own school.

"My school is a ______________ ______________
in ______________ with ______________ // ______________

6. To practice pronouncing words clearly try saying the following sentences, including the two traditional English tongue twisters:

a) The manager of VW visited the clothes shop.

b) Today's the thirteenth, we go on holiday on the thirtieth.

c) The ragged rascal ran round the rugged rock.

d) She sells seashells on the seashore. The shells that she sells are the sea-shells she saw.

Eine eigene Meinung ausdrücken *(Expressing an opinion)*

Die folgenden Redewendungen eignen sich sehr gut, um in einem Gespräch deine Meinung deutlich zu machen. Lerne sie auswendig.

I (would) prefer … *Ich würde lieber …*	→	I would prefer not to … *Ich würde lieber nicht …*
I (would) like … *Ich würde / möchte gern …*	→	I don't like / I dislike … *Ich würde nicht gern …*
I think / believe / expect / imagine / suppose (that) … *Ich glaube (dass) …*	→	I don't think (that) … *Ich glaube nicht (dass)…*
I doubt (that) … *Ich bezweifle (dass) …*	→	I don't doubt (that) … *Ich bezweifle nicht (dass) …*
I'm for … *Ich bin für … / dafür, dass …*	→	I'm against … *Ich bin gegen … / dagegen, dass …*
I would … *Ich würde …*	→	I wouldn't … *Ich würde nicht …*
I'm sure / certain… *Ich bin sicher …*	→	I'm not sure / certain … *Ich bin nicht sicher …*
In my opinion … *Meiner Meinung nach …*	→	That's not my opinion. *Das ist nicht meine Meinung.*

7. Join in this conversation about consumer habits and express your opinions clearly. A choice of good phrases to use for each situation is given in brackets together with a suggestion of what to say. Make your replies as long as possible giving details or examples.

YOU: How much money do you get each week?

ANNE: Not that much. My dad puts €40 a month into my bank, then he gives me another €5 a week.

YOU: *(I think / don't think – Bekommt Anne viel Taschengeld? Was hältst du von der Art und Weise, wie sie es bekommt?)*

____

____

____

ANNE: What do you do with your money? I like to buy CDs or things for my computer. But usually it just sits in the bank. I forget about it. What about you?

YOU: *(I like / I would – Was machst du mit deinem Geld?)*

____

____

ANNE: If my parents gave me more money, I doubt I would spend it – but I wouldn't say no!

YOU: *(I doubt / I'm sure / I think – Was ist deine Reaktion auf Annes Kommentar?)*

____

____

____

ANNE: Older people always say we've got too much money, what do you think?

YOU: *(In my opinion / I believe / I don't think – Beantworte Annes Frage so umfassend wie möglich.)*

____

____

____

ANNE: Sometimes I feel under pressure to buy things. Do you know what I mean? Clothes, I-pods – just so that I've got them as well.

YOU: *(I prefer / In my opinion / I think / I like / I believe – Was meinst du dazu, dass man bestimmte Dinge nur kauft, weil Freunde sie haben? Führe deine Antwort aus und gib Beispiele.)*

____

____

____

8. Look carefully at the photograph of the horse guard and read the short text. Then express your opinion about the horse guard: for example, about his job, what he might think about, and whether or not you would do it.

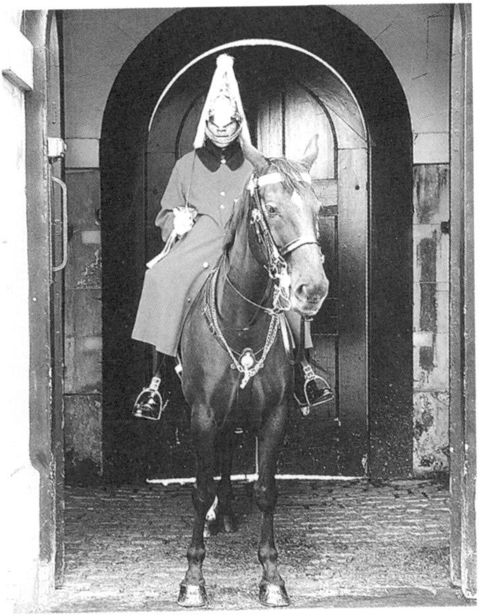

The horse guard must sit on his horse in all weathers, hot, cold, rain or snow. He is not allowed to talk to anyone nor move, except to exercise his horse by taking a few steps forward and then backwards again. In front of the guard there is a pavement which is about three or four metres wide and then a very busy main road in London that goes from Trafalgar Square to the Houses of Parliament. There are always many tourists in this area. They like to have their photographs taken with the horse guard and often stroke the horse. The horse guard, however, must remain still while on his one-hour duty and ignore the people around him.

9. Give your opinion about the topics in the list. Before you begin make notes about what you want to say. Use different ways to express your opinion.

a) The royal family in Britain

b) Looking after the environment

c) Sport on television

d) The European Union and its expansion

Andere nach ihrer Meinung fragen
(Asking other people for an opinion)

In einem Gespräch ist es nicht nur wichtig, seine eigene Meinung angemessen äußern und vertreten zu können. Ganz entscheidend ist es auch, andere Gesprächsteilnehmer nach ihrer Meinung zu fragen. Die folgenden Redewendungen helfen dir dabei. Lerne auch sie auswendig.

What's your opinion / view / reaction (about) ...?	→	*Was ist deine Meinung zu ...? / Was denkst du über ...?*
How do you see / view the situation / this?	→	*Wie siehst du die Situation?*
Could you explain something / your ideas / your feelings to me?	→	*Könntest du mir etwas erklären?*
What would you say about ...?	→	*Was würdest du über / zum Thema ... sagen?*
How do you feel about ...?	→	*Was hältst du persönlich von ...?*
(stark) What about (for example: no smoking in public places)? Do you think that's right?	→	*Was denkst du über ...? Glaubst du, dass das richtig / in Ordnung ist?*
(stark, eine Antwort fordernd) I don't suppose you'll / you would agree, will you / would you?	→	*Du wirst sicher nicht zustimmen, oder?*

Du kannst auch Fragen mit Verneinungen stellen, um deinen Gesprächspartner zu einer Meinungsäußerung zu bringen:

Don't you think that ...?	→	*Glaubst du nicht, dass ...?*
Wouldn't you like to see ...?	→	*Hättest du nicht auch lieber ...?*
Shouldn't we ...?	→	*Sollten wir nicht ...?*

10. Zoos are quite controversial. Some people think they are cruel, others think they are a good idea. Look at the photograph of a typical scene in one. Ask someone their opinion of zoos in **five** different ways.

11. Give your view of the following situations about cultural differences and then ask for someone else's opinion.

a) In Northern Ireland many working-class people are still segregated by religion. They live in Catholic or Protestant areas and their children go to Catholic or Protestant schools.

b) Many people leave their home countries to live in another. Some of these people do so because of their work, others do so to have better lives and some do so to escape persecution. Today, almost all European countries have problems with illegal immigration and asylum seekers.

c) Groups of foreign workers often form ghetto-like areas. They do this for many reasons: to feel safe, to have friends who speak the same language and have the same culture, or to be part of a community. However, multi-cultural societies do not mean integrated ones.

d) Even within Europe there are many cultural differences. In Britain, for example, people open their Christmas presents on 25th December and they have special celebrations, such as Guy Fawkes Night on 5th November. Foreigners living in a different country always have two cultures. Their own and their host nation's.

Zustimmen und widersprechen *(Agreeing and disagreeing)*

Um jemandem zu widersprechen, werden im Englischen häufig feststehende Redewendungen gebraucht, denn man möchte in seiner Ablehnung nicht zu kritisch bzw. schroff wirken. Einige dieser Redewendungen findest du hier. Außerdem sind einige Formulierungshilfen aufgelistet, die Zustimmung ausdrücken. Auch diese Redewendungen musst du wieder auswendig lernen.

I agree (with you). *Ich bin deiner Meinung.*	→	(I'm sorry but) I disagree (with you). *Ich bin nicht deiner Meinung.*
Yes, of course. *Ja, natürlich.*	→	No, not at all. *Nein, ganz und gar nicht.*
That's a good idea. *Das ist ein guter Vorschlag.*	→	(Excuse me but I think) That's a bad idea. *Das ist kein guter Gedanke / keine gute Idee.*
I'm for that. *Ich bin dafür.*	→	(I'm afraid) I'm against that. *Ich bin dagegen.*
You're right (about / that ...). *Du hast Recht (mit / wenn du sagst, dass ...).*	→	(I'm sorry, but) you're wrong (about / that ...). *Das stimmt nicht.*

Wenn du entsprechende Adverbien vor *right*, *wrong* und *understand* stellst, wird deine Antwort sehr deutlich.

You are absolutely right. *Du hast völlig recht.*	→	You are totally wrong. *Du liegst völlig falsch.*
You fully understand. *Du verstehst vollkommen.*	→	I think you don't really understand (the problem). *Ich glaube, du verstehst (das Problem) überhaupt nicht.*

Wenn du dir mit deiner Meinung nicht sicher bist, verwende Ausdrücke wie:

I'm not sure / certain.
Ich bin nicht sicher.

12. Look at the statements below. How would you agree or disagree with each one? A spoken answer must be given although you may want to make notes before starting.

a) "I don't see anything wrong with eating fast food every day."

b) "If professional sports people are found to be taking drugs, I think that they should be banned from taking part in their sport for life."

c) "Young people, today, are addicted to their mobile phones. Just look around you – as soon as they come out of school or a shop they're texting someone. They can't live without them."

d) "A big problem of tourism is that it damages the environment. Planes cause pollution; ski slopes damage the mountains; hotels, swimming pools and golf courses use too much water in areas where there's not a lot."

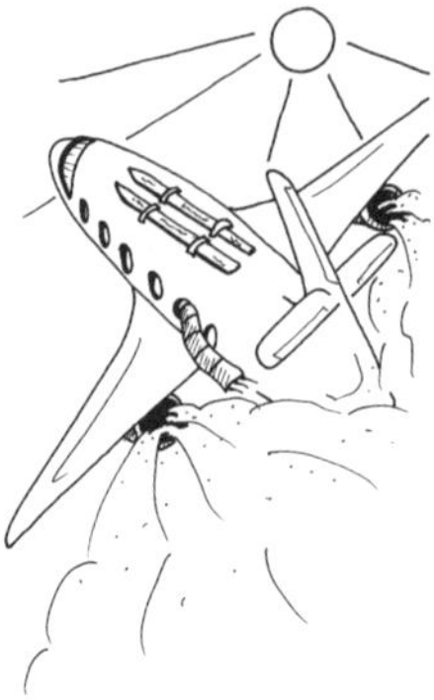

____

____

____

____

____

____

e) "Lots of young people, today, don't take enough exercise. They don't walk or cycle to school and they just sit at home watching television or playing computer games. They eat too much and drink too many fizzy drinks."

____

____

____

____

____

____

____

13. What points do you agree with or disagree with in this newspaper letter? Expand your reply as much as possible.

LETTERS TO THE EDITOR

Sir,

If I had behaved like some of the young people I see every day I would have been told off – not by my parents but by any adult who saw me misbehaving. But what happens today? People see kids misbehaving and just walk past as if they hadn't seen anything.

Yob culture is growing in our society. What do I mean by yob culture? I mean kids that behave badly, kids who don't care about other people or things around them, kids who would rather drop litter on the floor next to a waste bin or kick it over just for fun, kids who can't put two or three words together without swearing and can't remember when they last used 'please' or 'thank you' as synonyms for their Neanderthal grunts.

I don't mind faces held together with safety pins. Pink, yellow and green hair adds colour to a grey November day. But what does it cost to be nice?
Kind regards, Jane Smith

14. Read the newspaper report carefully. Agree or disagree with it.

SPECIAL REPORT

Poverty is terrible. We should all find time to do as much as we can for the poor people in the world. There have been many fund-raising events organised through the music industry, for example, and attempts by individuals and other organisations to alter things. However, the disadvantage of fund-raising events is that people are happy to buy what they are supposed to, or give money to it, but they quickly forget about the problem they are supporting, too. Most people prefer to be passive carers rather than getting actively involved in projects to help change things. Industries and consumers, though, could do more to fight poverty. If industries adopted more fair trading[1] policies, that is paying people a fair price for what they grow or manufacture, for example, then it would help many families who at the moment are exploited. Consumers should be made more aware of where the products come from and under what conditions they are made or grown. But it is no use just giving poor countries money. They need help to make positive changes so that they can learn to help themselves.

1 fair trading – the policy of trading in a fair way with third-world contries.

Jemanden unterbrechen *(Interrupting someone)*

Hier sind einige Ausdrücke, die du verwenden kannst, wenn du der Aussage eines Gesprächspartners zustimmen oder widersprechen willst. Deine Antwort sollte so ausführlich wie möglich sein.

Can I ask you something?	→	*Kann ich dich etwas fragen?*
Can / May I (just) say something, please?	→	*Kann ich bitte etwas sagen?*
Excuse me, but …	→	*Entschuldigung, aber …*
I don't wish / I'm sorry to interrupt / stop you but …	→	*Ich möchte dich nicht unterbrechen, aber … / Ich unterbreche dich ungern, aber …*
I'm sorry, I don't agree with …	→	*Ich bin anderer Meinung (als) …*
I'm sorry, that's not right / fair …	→	*Das ist nicht richtig / fair …*
I'm sorry, but (I'd just like to say) …	→	*Es tut mir leid, aber …*

Manchmal möchtest du jemanden unterbrechen, weil du eine ausgeprägte Meinung zu dem hast, was gesagt worden ist. Die „Nettigkeiten" werden dann meist weggelassen und die Ausdrucksweise ist sehr viel direkter. Denke aber daran, dass du nicht zu emotional oder wütend werden darfst, denn sonst besteht die Gefahr, dass du die Kontrolle über deine Äußerungen verlierst und dann vielleicht Fehler machst, die dir sonst nicht unterlaufen würden.

(*stark*) You're wrong there.	→	*Du hast nicht Recht. / Da hast du mit Sicherheit nicht Recht.*
I don't think you're / That's not right.	→	*Ich glaube, dass du nicht Recht hast.*
(wütend) Oh, come on! You don't really believe that.	→	*Das glaubst du doch selber nicht.*
How can you say that?	→	*Wie kannst du das sagen?*

15. Kim and Simon are dominating the group discussion about lifestyles. The asterisks (*) show you where you can say something. Interrupt the conversation and expand what you want to say as much as possible.

Example:

SIMON: I don't know why people complain about the environment and global warming. I think it's probably just a weather phase. You don't … (*)

Possible interruption:

YOU: <u>Oh, come on, Simon</u>! <u>How can you say that</u>? Just look at all the storms we keep having. You can't just say that these are only weather phases. Everyone knows that the world's climate is changing because of us – you know, the people who live in it and abuse it – me, you and the other millions of people.

a) KIM: I don't see anything wrong with our lifestyles today, we have everything we want and we can do most things …

SIMON: But that's the whole point Kim. We can do whatever we want, we've got the money and the opportunities to do so, but what about all the poor people?

KIM: To be honest, it's an 'I'm alright world' where we live. I don't like it but there's not a lot I can do about it. I'm not about to give up my computer, my bike, my CDs or my mobile phone just because other people don't have them. I … (*)

YOU: …

b) KIM: I can imagine in a few years' time that our lifestyles will be very different. The world is changing so fast. Already we're worrying about oil, we know that we're heavily polluting the world, we're starting to see the effects of climatic change – storms and floods everywhere. I think we need action now. I wish governments were much stronger in this and forced people to change. Why not increase the tax on petrol, for example? It would stop people using cars! Why not make car parking charges more expensive and the buses free? You've got to be hard, if you want change. You've … (*)

YOU: …

c) SIMON: My mum was telling me about when she was young. You always think things never really change but they do. She was saying that when she was at school, about our age, then life was a lot different.

KIM: Yeah, my parents do the same sometimes. My dad grew up without a television. His family didn't get one till he was 12 – can you imagine, no telly till you're twelve?

SIMON: Mum said they never had a phone, either. No, phone! I wouldn't know what to do. Think of all the times we just phone friends for nothing. 'Hi, Sue, have you got the answer to question 5?' – 'Do you fancy coming round to my place?' – You know, that sort of thing. I really think our parents had a tough life although they never … (*)

YOU: …

16. Jenny likes talking a lot. Interrupt what she says where the asterisks are. Try to select the best phrase to do this. The words in brackets give you some help about what to say; expand what you say as much as possible.

"Did I tell you that I'd been in Australia in the summer?" *(* – Wo?)*

"Adelaide and then all over. It was great but the flight took ages. I hate flying but you can only worry about it for so long, after that you don't care anymore. Anyway, Australia. The people are really friendly but most that you meet are white. Did you know many convicts were sent to Australia from Britain?" *(* – Warum?)*

"I'm not really sure, but what is sad is that the Aborigines were so badly treated in the past. Many of them have lost their way of life for good. Their 'family' is important to them and these links have been broken, too." *(* – Was bedeutet ‚family'?)*

"'Family' for the Aborigines is more what we would think of as a tribe. All over Australia you could find Aboriginal art and craft work. It's sold mainly to tourists – me, for example, I bought loads of things." *(* – Deiner Meinung nach ist es nicht richtig, dass Aborigines keine richtigen Berufe haben.)*

"Well, many do have real jobs – these are real jobs – but unemployment among the Aborigines is very high. It's important to buy from them, so they can live – that's my opinion, at least." *(* – Drücke deine Empörung darüber aus, wie die Aborigines in der Vergangenheit behandelt worden sind.)*

"There's prejudice everywhere – the Maoris in New Zealand, for example, but in Australia something is really being done for them – I think that's the same in New Zealand, as well."

Darum bitten, dass etwas wiederholt wird
(Asking for something to be repeated)

Wenn man in einer fremden Sprache mit jemandem spricht, versteht man leicht etwas falsch. Der Gesprächspartner redet vielleicht zu schnell, man wird von jemandem abgelenkt oder man denkt über den eigenen Redebeitrag nach und verliert dadurch den Faden der Unterhaltung. Hier sind einige Formulierungshilfen, mit denen du jemanden bitten kannst, etwas zu wiederholen, das er gerade gesagt hat. Du musst die Formulierungen natürlich an die jeweilige Situation anpassen.

Excuse me, could you say that again, please?	→	*Kannst du das bitte noch einmal sagen?*
Sorry, could you repeat that / what you said about …?	→	*Kannst du das bitte wiederholen?*
I'm sorry / I'm afraid I didn't quite hear / catch / understand what you said. Could you say / repeat it again, please?	→	*Es tut mir leid, aber ich habe nicht genau verstanden, was du meinst (gesagt hast). Kannst du das bitte noch einmal sagen?*
I'm sorry / I'm afraid I missed / forgot what you were saying (about …). Could you explain it again / once more, please?	→	*Es tut mir leid, ich habe nicht verstanden, was du (über …) gesagt hast. Kannst du mir das noch einmal erklären?*
I'm sorry / I'm afraid you were talking a bit too fast for me – could you say it again a little bit slower / would you mind repeating what you said, please?	→	*Es tut mir leid, du hast für mich etwas zu schnell gesprochen. Könntest du das bitte etwas langsamer wiederholen? / Es tut mir leid, das war ein wenig zu schnell für mich. Könntest du es bitte etwas langsamer wiederholen?*

17. What is the best way to ask someone to repeat what they have been saying in the following situations?

a) The speaker has been talking too fast.
b) The speaker gave a lot of information.
c) You didn't hear what the speaker said because your neighbour spoke to you.
d) You didn't hear the speaker because a lorry drove by noisily outside.
e) You want a few seconds to think about what the speaker has just said and formulate a reply in your head.

18. Karen is explaining about the Queen's private house in England. She has also brought a few photographs to show your group. Ask her to repeat what she said about the underlined sections of her talk now that she has finished.

"Sandringham is the most informal of all the Queen's private homes. The house was bought in the middle of the 19th century by Queen Victoria's eldest son, who later became Edward VII, and was re-built by him in 1870. It has beautiful gardens around it but it's more than just a country home of the royal family. It's an estate. An English estate means a business based around the land. Sandringham has farming, woodland and a sawmill,

pheasants, orchards, the Queen's stud where she breeds horses and, of course, tourism. The house is often used by the royal family but when they are not there you can wander through a few of the rooms where they sit and eat. It also has a wonderful museum containing many of their old cars.
You can easily recognise the houses and villages owned by the Queen which belong to the estate. Many of them are very nice country cottages, as in the photo, but it's the pale blue doors that show they belong to the Queen's estate. Whole villages can be seen with doors painted this unusual colour. As machines have taken over much of the work on the estate there's no longer a big need for estate workers' cottages so when they become empty, the Queen often sells them – then the doors are quickly repainted by the new owners."

a) Wie ist der Name des Hauses?
   Example: "I'm sorry I didn't quite catch the name of the Queen's private house. Could you repeat it, please?"
b) Wer hat das Haus wann gebaut?
c) Was für ein Unternehmen gibt es dort?
d) Wie erkennt man die zum Gut gehörenden Häuser?
e) Warum ist was passiert?

19. You are having an interview *(Vorstellungsgespräch)* for a part-time job. The manager of the supermarket speaks very quickly and not very clearly. You have a problem understanding him. Ask him to repeat what he has said where the asterisks (*) are. What you need repeated is in the brackets.

MANAGER: I'll just tell you quickly about the job. I need someone for two evenings a week after school – from 4 o'clock to 8 o'clock. And at the weekends … (*)
YOU: *(Welche Zeiten?)*

MANAGER: 4–8. But at the weekends I need you from 10 to 4. You get breaks, of course, and half an hour for lunch – half an hour's enough, there's not much to do around here. You'll be stacking shelves, cleaning, throwing the rubbish away – anything that needs doing, you'll be doing it. (*)

YOU: *(Was sollst du tun?)*

MANAGER: Basically anything you're told to do. The pay's OK. I'll give you £3.50 an hour, so that'll work out about £105 a week. Not bad for someone your age, eh? (*)

YOU: *(zu schnell gesprochen)*

MANAGER: I do talk too fast sometimes, even my wife has to ask me to repeat things. £105 a week – right, when can you begin – Monday? Thursday? At the weekend? I need to know for the paperwork. It's John, isn't it? (*)

YOU: *(Wann kannst du anfangen?)*

MANAGER: Monday, Thursday or at the weekend – let's say Saturday.

Ein bereits behandeltes Thema aufgreifen
(Returning to an earlier topic)

Manchmal kann eine Unterhaltung in der Gruppe sehr schnell von einem Thema zum nächsten übergehen, ohne dass du Gelegenheit hattest, etwas zu sagen. Vielleicht hast du auch das Gefühl, dass ein Thema nicht ausreichend diskutiert worden ist, und möchtest es noch einmal aufgreifen.

You said earlier …	→	*Du hast vorhin gesagt …*
You mentioned / talked about …	→	*Du hast … erwähnt.*
Returning to an earlier point / what you said about …	→	*Wenn ich noch einmal aufgreife, was du über / zum Thema … gesagt hast, …*
A few minutes ago you said …	→	*Vor ein paar Minuten hast du gesagt …*
As you said before …	→	*Wie du vorher / schon gesagt hast, …*
Can we go back to … for a minute?	→	*Können wir noch einmal auf … zurückkommen?*

20. What would you say to return to the underlined topics? Use different expressions and expand what you want to say as far as possible.

Example:

Situation: Everyone has talked about their holidays except you. Suddenly, the conversation is now about flying. But you had a fantastic holiday and could have talked a lot about it.

Possible solution: "You talked about holidays before, can I tell you about mine, too? It was great …"

a) The speaker has talked a lot about tennis and is now talking about other types of sport.

b) Your friends have had a lively discussion about their favourite bands but you couldn't say anything because of them. They are now talking about films.

c) Your friend has been giving his opinion about the press. He said they often do not give a true picture of events. He was angry because he always feels he is being lied to. Now he has started talking about politicians. You disagree with him about his view of the press.

d) You think that everyone has an equal chance to succeed but your group does not. They have spoken a lot about this topic. At the beginning, they talked about disadvantages in education because of home background but the conversation has now moved on. You feel there is still more to be said about the subject but you did not get the opportunity earlier to express your views.

e) Your group has just discussed young people being independent. They have now begun to talk about getting jobs. You know that in England when young people are 18 they are adults. That means their parents are no longer responsible for them. You want to explain this, and give your view about it, too.

21. You are a newspaper reporter asking questions about someone's speech on multicultural societies. Ask **five** good questions about what was said. Begin each question with a phrase that returns to the topic.

Example:

"You mentioned that England, especially, has been seen as a multicultural society for a long time. Why not Britain as a whole?"

Multicultural society in Britain

Britain, especially England, has been looked upon as a successful multicultural country for many decades now. The idea of multiculturalism was at first a good one. That was, to give everyone equal rights and not allow discrimination because of colour or religion. 'Foreign' people could then settle and integrate successfully into their new country. But the idea of multicultural societies has had its problems. The biggest one is that it has led to people of the same country of origin living closely together to create parallel societies; little Indias or little Pakistans, for example, where there is no need to learn English or the ways of the country.

In many of the traditional industrial areas of England, particularly in the West Midlands and Yorkshire, there are areas where there're hardly any white faces to be seen. The local residents speak their own languages and English for many school children is a foreign one.

It's understandable why people of the same foreign country like to be together. Groups offer safety and friendship. People feel part of a community rather than alone and vulnerable, as an individual in a foreign country does.

Many of the early immigrants into Britain are now grandparents and are retiring. A third generation of immigrants are now living in the country. Many of them are happy being British and are accepted as that. In some cases, though, there's still a cultural problem. In many families the culture of their grandparents still influences how the family lives. The young people of immigrant families, of course, now frequently find themselves in the middle of two opposing cultures.

22. Tom and Jenny are monopolising the conversation. Now they have stopped talking, how can you return to the underlined points? Take the opportunity to expand what you want to say as much as possible. (Theme: comics and cartoons)

JENNY: I really like newspaper cartoons. There're always fun – I often look at them first, before reading the paper!

TOM: I do, too. Sometimes it's easier to see the <u>cartoonist's opinion</u> than reading a long article.

JENNY: The point is, cartoonists can do what they want and no one cares. I've never heard of anyone getting upset about a cartoon – have you?

TOM: No, I haven't. But I remember reading that politicians sometimes buy the original of a cartoon, if it's something they really like.

JENNY: That'd be fun – collecting cartoons – especially about yourself.

TOM: <u>Embarrassing</u>, I'd say.

JENNY: Did you ever see Spitting Image, Tom?

TOM: No, I didn't. What was that?

JENNY: Shame, Spitting Image was great. It was a satire about people in the news using puppet-type caricatures of them. They weren't just politicians, but also well-known people – pop stars and so on.

TOM: I don't think I've watched anything like that but I guess many cartoons have a message. I remember reading that there were lots in Peanuts. That was really interesting.

JENNY: A lot of comics and cartoons have hidden messages, Tom, especially the better ones. Good against bad or role models for the young. You know – what's right, what's wrong, that sort of thing. They're quite clever really.

TOM: Yeah, we had to do a project in Art about comics. It was fun but hard work. We had to choose a famous person and then outline their life. I took Nelson Mandela. The hardest thing was to draw the same head at different angles. But you don't always need the whole figure. If you look at a comic, you see that often there's just a hand or part of a figure in a picture. You've got to remember that each picture is like a finished piece of artwork.

JENNY: That reminds me, do you know Roy Lichtenstein? He was an artist in the 60s who painted pictures like the ones from comics. They're great.

YOU: …

a) cartoonist's opinion
b) embarrassing
c) satire about people in the news
d) project in Art about comics

Das Thema wechseln *(Changing the subject)*

In jeder Diskussion gibt es einen Zeitpunkt, zu dem das Thema erschöpft ist. Niemand weiß mehr etwas zu sagen und es entsteht entweder ein peinliches Schweigen oder eine gezwungene Unterhaltung. In einer solchen Situation bietet es sich an, das Thema zu wechseln. Dabei ist es besser, die Führungsrolle zu übernehmen, als andere ein Diskussionsthema bestimmen zu lassen, das einen vielleicht nicht interessiert. Die im Folgenden aufgeführten Formulierungshilfen werden dir in dieser schwierigen Situation sicherlich gute Dienste leisten.

We've talked a lot about … Could we look at … now?	→	*Wir haben viel über … geredet. Könnten wir jetzt über … sprechen?*
Can we move on and talk about …?	→	*Können wir weitergehen und über … reden?*
We should really talk about … too.	→	*Wir sollten wirklich auch über … reden.*
That's my opinion about (e.g. tennis). But what about (e.g. football)? What do you think about it?	→	*So denke ich über … Aber was meinst du zu …?*
Can we talk about ... now?	→	*Können wir jetzt über … sprechen?*
Perhaps we should also talk about …	→	*Vielleicht sollten wir auch über … reden.*
Can / May I say something at this point?	→	*Kann ich an dieser Stelle etwas sagen?*

23. Change each topic of conversation to the new one. Expand what you say as far as possible.

Example:
food → holidays
"Can we move on – I'm getting hungry – and talk about holidays. I'd a great time in England – and the food wasn't too bad! Just a joke. England wasn't what I'd expected. The people were really friendly …"

a) immigrants → emigrants
b) Britons → Americans
c) religion → the royal family
d) being a vegetarian → addiction to drugs
e) poverty → consumer habits
f) global warming → mass tourism

24. In your group Kevin and Susie are always talking about what *they* want to. Change the topic of conversation into something that *you* would prefer to talk about. This may not be a complete change of subject, it could also be just to a different point of the original one that interests you more. Expand what you say as far as possible.

a) Theme: sport
KEVIN: I like sport a lot. I play football in a team on Tuesdays and then at the weekend I play handball, too. I don't understand people who don't do anything at all. What about you? Do you do anything?
YOU: …

b) Theme: advertising

SUSIE: I hate buying magazines when all you get are lots of adverts. The last one I got had twenty pages of adverts and only a few articles. I get really angry about it. It's not fair – €4 for a magazine just to have adverts!

YOU: …

c) Theme: respect

KEVIN: At school it's hard to be respected by other people. Lots of my friends try to dress cool so they get the respect of other people – 'Hey, he's cool', that sort of thing. But I think that's just show. Respect is something else. I don't respect everyone – some people just have my respect because of how they are as a person. It's difficult to explain. But if, say, a teacher tells me off for doing something I shouldn't have done, I can still have respect for him.

YOU: …

d) Theme: consumer habits

SUSIE: I love going out on Saturdays with my friends and looking around the shops. We go into clothes shops and just try things on for fun. I usually end up buying something, though. Last week I got a few T-shirts. One was great. It had 'I'm perfect' on it – that's me – perfect!

YOU: …

e) Theme: crime

KEVIN: I agree with the idea of zero tolerance. Zero tolerance is where if you break a law you get punished. There's no exception. This idea was introduced in New York and was very successful. It made New York into a much safer place than before and has reduced crime a lot. Some cities in England are also doing this. If you don't do anything wrong, there's nothing to worry about.

YOU: …

Andere zum Reden bringen *(Making people talk)*

Manchmal gerät die Unterhaltung ins Stocken, z. B. wenn niemand weiß, was er noch sagen könnte. Am einfachsten kann man Menschen zum Sprechen bringen, indem man eine direkte Frage an einen Einzelnen oder eine allgemeine Frage an die ganze Gruppe stellt. Englische Muttersprachler verwenden zu diesem Zweck häufig Bestätigungsfragen *(question tags).*

Direkte Fragen mit Fragewörtern: what, where, when, who, which, how		
What do you think, (Anne)?	→	*Was meinst du …?*
Entscheidungsfragen		
Are you interested in …?	→	*Interessierst du dich für …?*
Do you want a Europe …?	→	*Willst du ein Europa …?*
Bestätigungsfragen		
The weather is terrible today, isn't it?	→	*Das Wetter ist schrecklich, oder?*
Es können auch verneinte Fragen gebildet werden:		
Don't we all have a right (to be equal)?	→	*Haben wir nicht alle ein Recht …?*
Wouldn't you rather (have comprehensive education)?	→	*Wäre dir … nicht lieber?*
Shouldn't … / Couldn't … / Aren't … / Isn't … ?	→	*Sollte nicht … / Könnte nicht … / Sind nicht … / Ist nicht …?*

25. Imagine that you are in a group discussion. Formulate *five direct questions* that you could ask to create a conversation about each of the following topics. Expand what you say as far as possible on the theme of 'the school day'.

Example: "In my opinion afternoon lessons aren't very successful because pupils start to feel tired and lose concentration. What do you think (Peter)?"

a) The size of classes.
b) The workload at school.
c) The opportunities that are available.
d) The use of technology in the classroom.
e) School rules.
f) Social life within the framework of school.

26. Look at the photograph. How could you get people in your group to talk about the subject of public demonstrations? Give <u>five</u> examples of how this can be done.

27. How could you stimulate the conversation in the following situations?

a) The theme is young people's rights but no one really knows how to begin.

b) You have talked a lot about Australia and the Aborigines. There is not a lot more anyone can say. Can you link what you have been saying to New Zealand and get people to start talking again?

c) Many people, today, think that obesity in young people is rising dramatically. Your group has talked about exercising, diets and good eating habits. The conversation has now stopped. Can you get it going again? No one has mentioned the influence of other people yet: parents and other role models, for example.

d) Everyone has got something to say about smoking; and it looks like everyone has. Can you think of something original to say about this theme and get people to start talking more about what you have said?

2 Wie gehe ich mit Materialien in der Vorbereitungszeit um?

Bevor du in die mündliche (Gruppen-)Prüfung gehst, hast du eine Vorbereitungszeit von 15 bis 20 Minuten. Dein Lehrer legt dir Material (z. B. einen Text, ein Foto, eine Karikatur, eine Statistik) mit Fragestellung(en) vor. Dieses Material kannst du in der zur Verfügung stehenden Vorbereitungszeit unter den angegebenen Fragestellungen bearbeiten. Meist darfst du dir auch Notizen machen und diese in die Prüfung mitnehmen. Wie du mit dem Material und den Fragestellungen umgehen kannst, erfährst du hier.

Das Thema analysieren *(Analysing the theme)*

Zu jedem Diskussionsmaterial kannst du normalerweise die folgenden allgemeinen Punkte herausarbeiten.

- **Theme (Thema):** Wie lautet das Thema?
- **Main points (Hauptpunkte):** Welches sind die wichtigsten Punkte, die angesprochen werden?
- **Comments (Kommentare):** Was kannst du zu den Hauptpunkten sagen?
- **Opinion (Meinung):** Was ist deine Meinung (z. B. Standpunkte / zustimmen / widersprechen / Kompromiss)?
- **Focus (Eingrenzung):** Welche Einzelaspekte des Themas interessieren dich? (Konzentriere dich auf diese Punkte!)
- **Wider thinking (Zusammenhang):** Stelle das Thema in einen größeren Zusammenhang (z. B. Auswirkungen, Bedeutung).
- **Experiences (persönliche Erfahrung):** Kannst du in Bezug auf dieses Thema auf persönliche Erfahrungen zurückgreifen?
- **General knowledge (Allgemeinwissen):** Hast du Allgemeinwissen zu diesem Thema?
- **Questions (Fragen):** Bereite fünf Fragen zu dem Thema vor, die das Gespräch voranbringen können!

28. Read the short text then analyse the theme. A start has been made for you.

The long wait

The eldest son of the British monarch has often had a difficult time. From the day he is born he has only one role in life, that is to be king. He has no choice about this unless he decides to abdicate* and leave the country for ever. The eldest son is always made the Prince of Wales. In the past, many Princes of Wales have been very unhappy people because they did not know what to do with their lives while they waited to be king. The present Prince of Wales, though, is not like that, he has started many projects and is active in them. He established the Prince's Trust, for example, which helps young people begin their own businesses and he has used environmentally friendly farming methods on his own farmlands to create a successful multi-million pound business which shows other people that farming does not have to mean killing the countryside with chemicals.

(* auf den Thron verzichten)

your notes

theme	*Prince of Wales*
main points	*boring life ...*
comments	*sad life ...*
opinions	*eldest child should be heir ...*
focus	*abdication ...*
wider thinking	*is the monarchy needed?...*
experiences	*friends having to take over parents' businesses ...*

general knowledge	*monarchy ...*
questions	*How would you feel if your future was already planned out by someone else?...*

Notizen anfertigen *(Discussion notes)*

Nachdem du allgemeine Aussagen zum Thema gemacht hast, kannst du dich den Einzelaspekten zuwenden. Dabei ist es hilfreich, wenn du dir zur Vorbereitung auf die Diskussionsrunde Notizen machst. Diese Notizen können aus einzelnen Wörtern oder aus kurzen Teilsätzen bestehen. Auf jeden Fall sollten deine Notizen die Informationen so kurz und genau zusammenfassen wie möglich.

- Fertige deine Notizen in einer gut strukturierten Form an (d. h. gut gegliedert oder auch als Mindmap).
- Notiere dir nur das Wichtigste.
- Lies in der Diskussion nicht direkt von deinen Notizen ab. Das wirkt sehr unsicher.

29. Make discussion notes about the following topics:

a) young people's behaviour

b) a typical weekend

c) advertising and sport

d) expanding the European Union

e) the future of institutions, such as the British Commonwealth or the UN

30. Use your notes from exercise 29 and talk about each subject. Try to speak for at least two minutes without stopping.

Variation 1: Work with a friend. Prepare separate notes about the given topics, then discuss them between you. Aim to speak for at least 10–15 minutes on each theme.

Variation 2: This could also be a group discussion. In this case extend the speaking time to 15–20 minutes.

Textmaterial *(Texts)*

Je nach Lesetext oder Aufgabenstellung gibt es unterschiedliche Vorgehensweisen. Manchmal musst du die Gesamtaussage des Textes erfassen *(reading for gist)* und manchmal sollst du Details aus dem Text herausfinden. Du musst dann den Text nach den geforderten Informationen durchforsten *(skimming* oder *scanning).*
Zunächst einmal ist es sinnvoll, den Text an sich ganz genau zu betrachten. Manchmal kannst du bereits am **Layout**, d. h. an der Gestaltung des Textes erkennen, um welche Textsorte es geht. Wenn du weißt, ob der dir vorliegende Text eine Werbeanzeige, ein Zeitungsartikel oder ein Interview ist, dann bist du schon einen Schritt weiter.
Als Nächstes solltest du den Text einmal **genau lesen**. Die meisten unbekannten Wörter kannst du ganz leicht aus dem **Sinnzusammenhang erschließen**. Lass dich also nicht aus der Ruhe bringen, wenn du das eine oder andere Wort nicht kennst. Ganz entscheidend ist, dass du dir bei diesem Arbeitsschritt einen guten Überblick über den Inhalt deines Textes verschaffst.
Nun solltest du die **Aufgabenstellungen genau lesen**, damit du weißt, unter welchen Aspekten du den Text bearbeiten sollst. Wenn du den Lesetext im Hinblick auf die Aufgabenstellungen liest, kannst du ganz gezielt wichtige **Schlüsselwörter bzw. Textpassagen markieren**, damit du sie bei der Bearbeitung der Aufgaben schnell wieder findest.

- Schaue dir den Lesetext genau an. Kannst du vom **Layout** auf die **Textsorte** schließen?
- Lies den Text genau durch und verschaffe dir so einen guten **Überblick über** den **Inhalt** des Textes.
- Lies die **Aufgabenstellungen** genau. Markiere beim nochmaligen Lesen des Textes wichtige Textaussagen im Hinblick auf die Aufgabenstellungen.
- Mache dir **Notizen** für die Diskussionsrunde.
- Denke an die **Sprechfertigkeiten**, die du auf den Seiten 3 bis 28 dieses Buches geübt hast (z. B. wie man andere nach ihrer Meinung fragt, wie man sie zum Sprechen bringt, wie man anderen widerspricht).
- Sei darauf vorbereitet, die **Gesprächsführung** zu übernehmen. Überlege dir beispielsweise Fragen, mit denen du andere zum Sprechen bringen kannst.

31. Read the text about the Irish Republic carefully.

The Republic of Ireland

'Poverty to wealth' could be a summary of Ireland's history. From being a country where people had no future and left, it has become one where they want to stay.

Ireland's struggle for independence from Britain began in 1916 with the Easter Rising but it was not until 1949 that the Republic of Ireland was formed. Ireland had always been a poor country and independence made no difference. People continued to leave Ireland to escape the poverty there, two of the many large problems the country faced: poverty and emigration. However, since the late 1990s Ireland has changed dramatically. Irish people no longer wanted to leave their country because the economy was booming, and other people started moving to Ireland for work instead.

During the 1980s and the 1990s Ireland was helped by the EU but later its economic growth was a result of people's own hard work. For the first time in Ireland's history a lot of people had a lot of money. This, though, has brought many disadvantages: new car sales have greatly increased but so has traffic congestion; house prices have doubled in seven years, making owners rich, but young people cannot afford to buy homes of their own.

Ireland now has low unemployment and there are many jobs available especially in the areas of technology. However, because many people are now moving to Ireland from all over the world, it is quickly developing into a multicultural society. Unfortunately, racism has become a new problem for Ireland, which is made worse by the increasing number of asylum seekers also arriving.

Young people are also changing. They have more money to spend because their parents are richer and there are many well-paid part-time jobs. However, the English disease of binge drinking – drinking a lot of alcohol very quickly – is happening and traditional Irish pubs, often the centre of communities, are now being replaced by theme pubs with doormen.

A lot of Irish people have mixed feelings about its new wealth. They say Ireland has lost its identity and its people now only think about money. They complain that the traditional characteristics of the nation – the warmth of the Irish welcome, sharing, being part of a community and their relaxed way of life – are all disappearing. Are these people simply romanticising about the past, or is it really all too much, too fast?

a) What do these words from the text mean in German?

poverty ______________________

wealth ______________________

struggle ______________________

(to be) formed ______________________

economy ______________________________

was booming ______________________________

economic growth ______________________________

available ______________________________

asylum seekers ______________________________

community ______________________________

b) Analyse the theme.

____

c) Make discussion notes on the following points about the Republic of Ireland. Aim to speak for at least two minutes on each topic without stopping.
   - Ireland's past problems
   - the worries of the Irish
   - having new money
   - racism
   - young people

   Variation 1: Work with a friend. Prepare separate notes about the given topics, then discuss them between you. Aim to speak for at least 10–15 minutes on each theme.

   Variation 2: This could also be a group discussion. In this case extend the speaking time to 15–20 minutes.

d) Although the following topics are connected to the text, you may talk freely about them. Make notes before you begin. Give your thoughts, experiences and your opinions where possible. Speak for at least three minutes on each topic.
   - too much, too fast
   - developing countries
   - asylum seekers
   - old ways and traditions versus modern living
   - integrated societies

   Variation 1: Work with a friend. Prepare separate notes about the given topics, then discuss them between you. Aim to speak for at least 10–15 minutes on each theme.

   Variation 2: This could also be a group discussion. In this case extend the speaking time to 15–20 minutes.

Bilder *(Photographs)*

Auch ein Bild oder Foto kann Ausgangspunkt einer Diskussion sein. Meistens wird von dir verlangt, das Bild zunächst einmal zu beschreiben. Anschließend soll das Bild interpretiert werden oder du wirst aufgefordert, das dargestellte Thema in einen größeren Zusammenhang zu stellen.

- Mache dir allgemeine **Notizen** zum Bild: Was siehst du auf dem Bild? Was stellt es dar?
- Welches **Thema** wird auf dem Bild angesprochen? Was soll es aussagen?
- Sprich in der Diskussion über deine **persönlichen Erfahrungen** zu diesem Thema.
- Beteilige andere am Gespräch, indem du beispielsweise gezielte Fragen stellst.
- Sprich über den Zweck von Fotografien für Nachrichten, die Erinnerung usw.
- Denke an die **Sprechfertigkeiten**, die du auf den Seiten 3 bis 28 dieses Buches geübt hast (z. B. wie man andere nach ihrer Meinung fragt, wie man sie zum Sprechen bringt, wie man anderen widerspricht).
- Sei darauf vorbereitet, die **Gesprächsführung** zu übernehmen.

32. a) Study the photograph carefully. Look how information can be found in it. Complete the missing information.
Background information: The photograph is taken at midday in Piccadilly Circus, London.

b) Analyse the theme of the photograph in general.

c) Ask yourself questions about the photograph. Give as much information as possible in note form about each question – some starting points have been given.
   - What do I know about London?
     congestion charge, ______________________________
   - Why are there so few vehicles?
     it's midday – there should be more, ______________________________
   - ______________________________
   - ______________________________
   - ______________________________
   - ______________________________

d) Discussion themes around this photograph could be, for example:
   - congestion in towns and cities
   - poverty and wealth
   - commuting
   - cars and the environment

   Make discussion notes about these themes. You can relate them, for example, to the photograph and your own experiences. Give your opinions, too. Talk about each topic for at least three minutes.

   Variation 1: Work with a friend. Prepare separate notes about the given topics, then discuss them between you. Aim to speak for at least 10–15 minutes on each theme.
   Variation 2: This could also be a group discussion. In this case extend the speaking time to 15–20 minutes.

33. 

a) Study the photograph carefully.
Background information: The photograph was taken at the East Side Gallery in Berlin, 2005, where a section of the former Berlin Wall remains and has been decorated by professional artists. Graffiti has since been added.

b) Make a general analysis of the theme. Talk about the photograph and the theme for at least three minutes.

c) The following points are connected to the photograph in some way but you may talk freely about them. Make discussion notes about each one. Expand what you say as far as possible. Aim to talk for at least three minutes about each topic.
- keeping things for history
- graffiti or freedom to express oneself
- political statements through the arts
- tourist attractions

Variation 1: Work with a friend. Prepare separate notes about the given topics, then discuss them between you. Aim to speak for at least 10–15 minutes on each theme.
Variation 2: This could also be a group discussion. In this case extend the speaking time to 15–20 minutes.

Karikaturen *(Cartoons)*

Karikaturen können ebenfalls Ausgangspunkt für ein Gespräch sein. Zunächst solltest du – genau wie bei anderen visuellen Impulsen – die Bildvorlage genau betrachten.

- Mache dir allgemeine **Notizen** zur Karikatur: Was siehst du? Was stellt die Karikatur dar?
- Welches **Thema** wird in der Karikatur angesprochen? Was soll sie aussagen?
- Sprich in der Diskussion über deine **persönlichen Erfahrungen** zu diesem Thema.
- Beteilige andere am Gespräch, indem du beispielsweise gezielte Fragen stellst.
- Sprich über den Zweck von Karikaturen – vor allem von politischen Karikaturen. Was hältst du von ihnen? Wie schätzt du ihren Wert ein? Hast du in jüngster Zeit eine Karikatur gesehen, die dir wirklich gut gefallen hat?
- Denke an die **Sprechfertigkeiten**, die du auf den Seiten 3 bis 28 dieses Buches geübt hast (z. B. wie man andere nach ihrer Meinung fragt, wie man sie zum Sprechen bringt, wie man anderen widerspricht).
- Sei darauf vorbereitet, die **Gesprächsführung** zu übernehmen.

34. government report of the school: on show, must be good

St Mary's – suggests church school

rows of books – academic feeling

probably the deputy headteacher

primary school

headteacher's office

'I see ... entirely without social skills, unable to speak properly, can't hold a knife and fork or do up buttons ... now, what about your child?'

undesirable, lower-class parents: fat, tattoos, unsuitably dressed, shoes undone, wrong image

headteacher: making notes about parents / pupil – selection process

headteacher's comment – suggesting parents are not acceptable (caption)

child – ready for school but looking unintelligent; cap on backwards, younger version of parents

notes about other children and their families on the floor and in the container: suggests too many applicants

a) Study the cartoon carefully.
Background information: Theoretically, parents can send their children to any school they want to in England. Some schools have a good name and others do not. The good schools are very popular and often have more children wanting to go to them than they can accept. Many of these schools are now selecting their pupils.

b) Using your notes describe the cartoon and what is happening in it. Talk for about two minutes.

c) Analyse the theme of the cartoon. Use your notes to talk about the theme.

theme	
main points	
comments	
opinions	
focus	
wider thinking	
experience	
general knowledge	
questions	

d) Possible discussion themes around this cartoon could be, for example:
- pupil selection by schools
- appearances count
- problem pupils
- measuring success
- education and money

Give two more discussion topics which would be suitable for the theme of the cartoon.

____

____

e) Make notes about the discussion themes. You can relate them, for example, to the cartoon and your own experiences. Give your opinions where possible, too. Talk about each topic for at least three minutes.

Variation 1: Work with a friend. Prepare separate notes about the given topics, then discuss them between you. Aim to speak for at least 10–15 minutes on each theme.
Variation 2: This could also be a group discussion. In this case extend the speaking time to 15–20 minutes.

35. Use the cartoon as a starting point for discussion.

'Nearly there ...wait for it ...wait for it'

a) Identify the main points in the cartoon and then talk about it for at least two minutes.

Background information – British people do not like being part of the EU. Some of their governments are pro-European, others are anti-European. The figures at the end of the rope are the Prime Minister at that time, Tony Blair, and leading members of his government team: the Chancellor of the Exchequer, George Brown, the Deputy Prime Minister, John Prescott, and the Foreign Minister, Jack Straw.

b) Analyse the theme of the cartoon. Talk about it for two minutes.

c) Make discussion notes about the following themes. You can relate them, for example, to the cartoon and your own experiences. Give your opinions where possible, too. Talk about each topic for at least three minutes.
   - cartoons and understanding politics
   - freedom of speech and expression
   - politicians and the people
   - the European Union

   Variation 1: Work with a friend. Prepare separate notes about the given topics, then discuss them between you. Aim to speak for at least 10–15 minutes on each theme.
   Variation 2: This could also be a group discussion. In this case extend the speaking time to 15–20 minutes.

d) Imagine that you are in a group discussion and the conversation is getting difficult because people do not know what to talk about. Give two questions for each topic which will help the conversation.

   For example: (cartoons and political understanding) Don't you agree, (Mike,) that cartoons make you see the problems in politics clearer?

Diagramme, Grafiken, Schaubilder *(Diagrams)*

Auch eine grafische Darstellung kann als Grundlage für ein Gespräch dienen. Zunächst solltest du – genau wie bei anderen visuellen Impulsen – die Vorlage genau betrachten.

- Mache dir allgemeine **Notizen** zur Grafik: Was siehst du? Was stellt die Grafik dar?
- Stelle einen Zusammenhang zwischen dem Schaubild (bzw. den darin enthaltenen Informationen) und dem Diskussionsthema her.
- Sprich in der Diskussion über deine **persönlichen Erfahrungen** zu diesem Thema.
- Beteilige andere am Gespräch, indem du beispielsweise gezielte Fragen stellst.
- Sprich über den Zweck von Schaubildern: Warum werden sie eingesetzt?
- Denke an die **Sprechfertigkeiten**, die du auf den Seiten 3 bis 28 dieses Buches geübt hast (z. B. wie man andere nach ihrer Meinung fragt, wie man sie zum Sprechen bringt, wie man anderen widerspricht).
- Sei darauf vorbereitet, die **Gesprächsführung** zu übernehmen.

36.

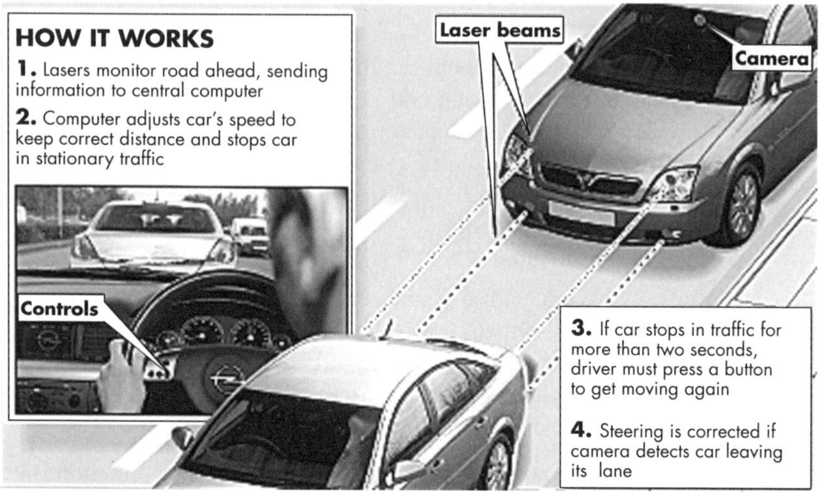

a) Study the diagram carefully. See how the important information is identified.
   - description of how it works
   - inside view of car
   - control panel; driver's view
   - car in front
   - car behind with controls
   - how the technology works

b) Analyse the theme of the diagram. A start has been made for you. Then talk about it for at least three minutes.

theme	*car technology*
main points	*car that controls itself in traffic by adjusting speeds, keeping distances and by stopping*
comments	
opinions	

focus	
wider thinking	
experience	
general knowledge	
questions	

c) Discussion themes around this diagram could be, for example:
- too much technology in everyday objects
- living in a technological world
- parents and technology – a generation gap?
- technology and social breakdown

Think of two more discussion topics which would fit the theme of the diagram.

____

____

d) Make notes about the discussion themes. You can relate them, for example, to the diagram, and your own experiences. Give your opinions where possible, too. Talk about each topic for at least three minutes.

Variation 1: Work with a friend. Prepare separate notes about the given topics, then discuss them between you. Aim to speak for at least 10–15 minutes on each theme.
Variation 2: This could also be a group discussion. In this case extend the speaking time to 15–20 minutes.

37.

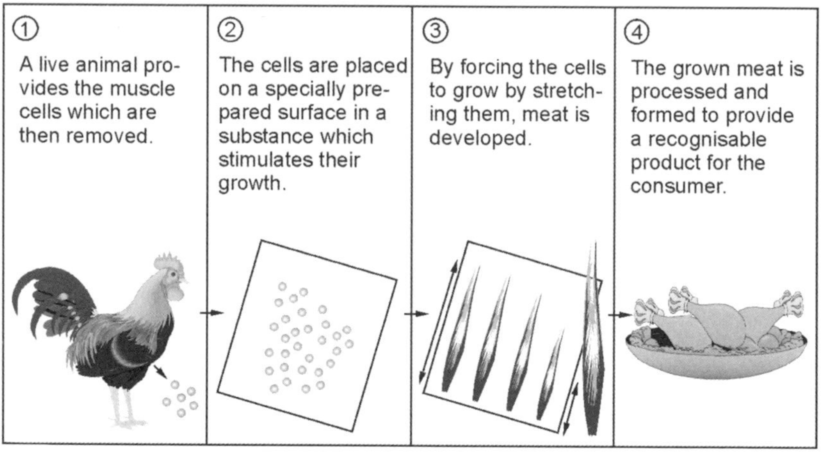

a) Study the diagram carefully. Identify the main points.

b) Analyse the theme of the diagram. Use your notes to talk about it for at least three minutes.

c) Make discussion notes about the following themes. Add <u>two</u> more topics to the list.
   - vegetarian dilemma: meat that doesn't live
   - the food we eat
   - cloning
   - providing for the Third World
   - ____
   - ____

d) Talk about each topic for at least three minutes.

e) Make up <u>two</u> questions for each discussion theme which you could ask someone.

   Variation 1: Work with a friend. Prepare separate notes about the given topics then discuss them between you. Aim to speak for at least 10–15 minutes on each theme.
   Variation 2: This could also be a group discussion. In this case extend the speaking time to 15–20 minutes.

3 Lösungsvorschläge

Note: In the key most 'answers' are examples of what you might say. Use them as a guide. They are also written in a style suitable for spoken rather than written English.

1. a) Yes, I do. I particularly like watching football and I enjoy playing handball. I think sport's very good for people because you're active and also because you get to know lots of people. You also get used to being part of a team and all that means, for example having responsibilities.

b) Yes, I think it is. I eat it without really thinking about what I eat. Sometimes I ask myself, 'What exactly is fast food?' OK, a burger is clear but I guess a Bratwurst is equally 'fast food' – what about a doner kebab or a pizza? Fast food has a lot of unhealthy things in it – fat, salt, sugar and so on – but if you eat this type of food occasionally, I'm sure it's not too bad for you.

c) Yes and No. I'm not sure, really. Sometimes I think it will be because of all the unemployment in Germany but then at other times I think that if a job is there I've just as much chance as anyone else to get it. I'll try hard to get a job as soon as I leave school and I'm prepared to move for one unlike some of my friends.

d) Yes, I would. I think it'd be really interesting to see how other people live. An exchange, for me, isn't just about language but about understanding other cultures, even simple things like what's for breakfast. I'd very much like to go away for a longer period, perhaps half a year or even a whole school year. I'm sure I'd gain a lot from the experience.

e) Yes, but not out of any thought for the animals that are killed. Sometimes I find myself choosing vegetarian meals when I can. I just like the taste of them. Anyway, I'm always a bit worried about all the things you read in the newspapers about meat products. I don't eat beef because of BSE and I'm not sure about chickens, and so on, because of antibiotics in their feed, and I don't like pork so there's not a lot left to eat, is there?

2. a) My father usually takes me to school in his car on his way to work. If I went by bus, I'd have to get up even earlier and everyone in the house would need to do things half an hour sooner, for example having breakfast. If my father can't drive me to school, then I'm too late to get the bus, so I have to use my bike instead, which is alright in summer but not much fun in winter.

b) I like reading our regional newspaper, the *Märkische Allgemeine*, because it has local news and sports results in it. It's also got information about what's on in the area, too, which I like. I can find out what's on at the cinema or if there's anything to do. I usually watch the news on television so I don't feel that I miss what's going on in the world just because I only read the local paper.

c) I've got a lot, really, but I like the magazine type programmes that show what's going on in the world. I like *Frontal 21*, for example, because it usually has interesting topics and the presentation is good.

d) That's a difficult question since I'd like to see as much as possible. However, if I could only select one place, I guess it would be Manhattan. I think this is really what America's about – skyscrapers, shops, the colourful way of life there ...

e) The school uniform is mainly black and green. The trousers and shoes are black, the jumper is green with a school logo on it. The shirt is white and the school tie has green, purple and silver stripes on it.

3. a) believe, expect, (to be) of the view, suppose, imagine ...

b) first, secondly, after that, next, later, afterwards, also, at the same time ...

c) said, explained, mentioned, spoke, recounted ...
trip, journey, holiday, stay ...

4.

(to) shout	scream / cry /yell
house	home
pupils	schoolchildren
(to) tell	say / explain
area	place / environment
tourists	visitors / holidaymakers
religion	belief / church
teenager	youth / young person
the newspapers	the press

5. My school is a typical secondary school in a large town with about 950 pupils. Many of the school's pupils come from nearby. Most people in the school either walk or come by bike in the mornings.

7. YOU: I think that's quite a lot. Most of my friends get less. I like the idea of your dad putting the money into your bank account. Mine just gives it to me every week – on Sunday, when I can't spend it!

YOU: I like to save my money. I'd prefer to go into town on Saturday and spend it too, but when you get it on Sunday you have to wait until the next weekend to buy something, then I think, 'Why not wait till next week because tomorrow I'll have more to spend'.

YOU: I'm sure you wouldn't! But I doubt that you wouldn't spend it, though. Maybe you'd save it, but then you'd just go and spend it on something else another day.

YOU: I don't doubt that we've got more money than they had. But then again it's our parents and relatives who give us the money. Or, if we've got a part-time job, we earn it. I don't believe there's anything wrong in having more money than they did or how we spend it. In my opinion older people are a little bit jealous of our generation because we can have a lot of things they couldn't.

YOU: I think that a lot of people feel under pressure to buy things, just like you. I want to believe that I don't get things just because my friends have them but sometimes you can't really help it. I'm certain if I had an old mobile phone, for example, my friends would laugh at me. I'm against this but it happens all the time. It's like with fashion, too. If you don't have the right trainers, or whatever, you're not cool. I don't like this but everyone does it because no one wants not to be cool.

8. I wouldn't like his job, in fact I think I would hate it. I can't see any fun in sitting on your horse for an hour in all sorts of weather and then have tourists around you all the time like annoying flies. I'd prefer to do anything rather than his job. However, I think he looks really good in his uniform and I'm sure he's proud of his job. It's just not for me. I can't imagine what he thinks about. I wonder why he's there, though, because if he has to ignore everyone, how can he guard properly when he should be looking at the people around him? I doubt that he's much more than a tourist attraction anyway.

9. a)

royal family

for
- important for Britain
- tourism
- show
- stability
- focus of attention
- tradition
- do good work

against
- too many of them
- old-fashioned
- out of touch
- cost a lot

b)

looking after the environment

- important
- pollution
- government's role
- organisations
- locally

- do more
- everyone should care
- world's role
- education
- nationally

c)

sport on television

for
- why not?
- balance of programmes
- sport channels
- sport is popular
- sport helps understanding

against
- too much
- minority interest
- takes up too much time
- not entertaining
- too much money spent on it

d)

the EU and its expansion

- is it necessary?
- trade
- loss of individuality
- business opportunities
- no borders – advantages / disadvantages

- where are the limits?
- loss of jobs in border areas
- good for poorer countries
- too big / expensive

10. a) Sometimes I feel sorry for the animals in zoos, but then it's nice being able to see them rather than just looking at photographs or films. What's your opinion?

b) What's your reaction to wild animals being placed in zoos? Don't you think it's cruel?

c) I like going to zoos and looking at all the animals there. I think zoos offer people the opportunity to get close to these animals without any danger. I don't suppose you'd agree, would you?

d) A lot of zoos help animals to survive. Many of them have been born in zoos and couldn't return to their natural habitat. What do you think about this point? Would you rather the animals be put back in the wild where they will die?

e) Don't you think it is better to have places where people can see wild animals, especially children, than never allowing them to see them? Not everyone can go on holiday to Africa.

11. a) I think it's terrible that people should be segregated by religion. We often talk about integration, especially of foreigners into our country, but in Northern Ireland they've got barriers just because of people's beliefs – probably not even beliefs, just their hate. But other countries are just as guilty of this to some extent. Look at us, we separate our religious studies in school – isn't this segregation? Shouldn't schools be bringing people together and not identifying them as being different?

b) I believe there's nothing wrong in people moving from one country to another because of work or to study. In fact, I think that there are many advantages in this. I realise, too, that many other people must flee their own country because of fear. What I don't understand, though, is how this problem is being dealt with. What about you, what's your opinion?

c) People from the same country have often grouped together when living abroad. Little Germanys and little Englands have always existed in foreign countries, and what about the Irish community in New York or the Chinese with their Chinatowns? I'm sure that these people did this so that they felt safe and welcomed. But, in my opinion, living in these types of communities has the disadvantage that people in them don't have to integrate with the native population. How do you feel about this?

d) I'm not sure that I would enjoy living with two cultures. On the one hand things like the Fourth of July in America would be fun but meaningless. And what about Christmas, for example? Would I open my presents on (the) 24th or (the) 25th? How do you feel about this? Would you open your presents on Christmas Eve or like everyone else in America, on Christmas morning?

12. a)

unhealthy fattening fast food at home education	**fast food daily**	silly opinion define fast food obesity social background

I'm sorry but I disagree with you. Eating fast food every day is certainly bad for you. (…)

b) illegal
banned
bad image
pressure to win

sport and drugs

cheating
punished severely
role models
accidental / deliberate

I agree. They know the rules and they know drugs are bad for you. (…)

c) safety
abused
social communication
technological world

young people and mobiles

why not?
texting
addiction
health risks

I disagree. Some people play with their phones all the time but most young people don't. (…)

d) damage
pollution: transport / waste
businesses

environment and tourism

resources
controls
balancing both
jobs

You're right, of course. But the problem is that if tourisms in these places didn't take place many people would be without jobs. (…)

e) obesity / poor diet
more sports interest
reflect wealthier society
education

unhealthy young people

education needed
lifestyle problem
technology: cars, phones computers
social background

I'm sorry but I totally disagree with you. Sure, some people do sit around all the time and eat too much but most of us don't. (…)

13. agree: stop bad behaviour and yob culture / stop swearing / too much unpleasantness / fashion is OK / costs nothing to be nice / everyone should try to stop young people behaving badly

disagree: people should try to stop bad behaviour but not put themselves at risk / don't think yob culture is increasing

I think Ms Smith is absolutely right when she comments upon the bad behaviour of many young people. But it's not all young people who act in this way. Most are really super and do nothing wrong. I'm certain that the problem lies with only a small minority who spoil the world for everyone. (…)

14. agree: terrible / help / fund-raising / people's memories are short / most people do not care after a while / responsible business / fair trade / consumer knowledge / money alone is not the answer / education

disagree: every contribution is important / people can't always help / people not in a position to change / help should be from governments

I'm not sure that I totally agree with what is said. Of course what is written is true. It's easy to say, for example, that people soon forget about poverty but concerts do raise a lot of money for charities. How much are individuals expected to do? (…)

15. a) YOU: I'm sorry but I don't agree with you. Just because it's an 'I'm alright world' doesn't mean that all you have to care about is yourself. You can actually do things for other people and you don't have to have the latest whatever just because everyone else has got it. (…)

b) YOU: I don't mean to stop you but I agree. Our lifestyles are harming the world. We've all got to do something but it needs governments to make real change. I think people only react when it costs them money. (…)

c) YOU: I'm sorry, but I don't agree with you. Our parents didn't have the things we do but that doesn't mean they had a harder life. Sometimes, I think their lives were easier – less hectic and stressful. (…)

16. I'm sorry but where exactly did you go?

Can I ask you something? Why did Britain send their convicts to Australia?

Excuse me, but what does 'family' mean?

I'm sorry to interrupt but don't you think it's wrong that the Aborigines can only live from tourism?

I don't want to stop you but I don't really agree. I find making and selling little souvenirs for tourists embarrassing. The Aborigines haven't been allowed to continue their own culture nor have they been accepted as equal. As a result they've never had the same chances as white Australians.

17. a) I'm sorry, you were talking a bit too fast for me, could you say it again but a little slower, please?

b) I'm sorry I didn't quite catch everything you said. Could you repeat it please?

c) I'm sorry, I missed what you were saying. Could you repeat it please?

d) I'm sorry, I didn't hear what you said because of the lorry. Could you say it again please?

e) I'm sorry I didn't quite understand what you said before; could you repeat it please?

18. a) I'm sorry I didn't quite catch the name of the Queen's private house. Could you repeat it, please?

b) I'm sorry, I missed what you were saying about who built the house and when; would you mind repeating it, please?

c) I'm afraid you were talking a bit too fast for me about the businesses on Sandringham Estate. Could you say it again a little slower, please?

d) Sorry, could you repeat what you were saying about how to recognise the houses?

e) I'm sorry I didn't quite understand why the houses become empty. Could you say it once more, please?

19. YOU: I'm sorry, could you repeat the times, please?

YOU: I'm sorry, could you explain again what I would be doing?

YOU: I'm afraid you were speaking a bit too fast for me. Could you say it again but a little bit slower, please?

YOU: I'm sorry, I didn't quite catch what you said about which days I could start working. Could you say them again, please?

20. a) Can we go back to tennis for a minute?

b) You talked earlier about favourite bands, can I tell you about mine, too? I didn't have the chance before.

c) You talked about your opinion of the press, I would like you to hear my opinion, too.

d) A few minutes ago you talked about the disadvantages in education but I think there's till more to be said.

e) Returning to what you said about being independent. Did you know that in England ...?

21. a) You said earlier that multicultural societies were a good idea which have failed. Could some other way to integrate immigrants have been more successful?

b) You talked about parallel societies but this happens all over the world where minorities settle. We don't criticise our little Germanys in South America for example, do we?

c) You mentioned that English for many children is a foreign language. What do the schools do about this?

d) As you said before, groups feel safe together. Can this ever be changed?

e) Can we go back to the cultural problems of the third generation immigrants? How bad is this culture clash and could you provide some examples?

22. a) A few minutes ago you mentioned cartoonists expressing their opinions. I think making fun of the news is important. It makes people think about very basic aspects of it and draws their attention to them. (…)

b) You said earlier that it'd be embarrassing collecting cartoons of yourself. I don't think it would. It'd be fun. I could imagine doing that, too. (…)

c) Can we go back to satire about people in the news? I don't think that's bad. It's good to laugh about situations and indirectly this brings these things to the attention of more people. (…)

d) You talked about making comics in Art. I wish we could do that. (…)

23. a) Perhaps we should also talk about emigrants.

b) Can we talk about Americans, now?

c) That's my opinion about religion. But what about the royal family? What do you think about them?

d) We've talked a lot about being a vegetarian. Could we look at addiction to drugs now?

e) Can we move on and talk about consumer habits?

f) May I just say something at this point? I think we should look at mass tourism, it's also got something to do with global warming but what I really want to say is …

24. a) YOU: Yes, I do. I like playing tennis but we've talked a lot about sport. Could we look at advertising now? You see that a lot in sport but also in other places too. (...)

b) YOU: I know it gets you angry, Susie, but can we move on and talk about what should be in magazines and not just about the ads?

c) YOU: Respect is important but so is trust. Can we talk about that now? Trust is really important when you deal with people. (...)

d) YOU: You, perfect! That's a joke! Seriously, though, can we talk about sport now? (...)

e) YOU: Can I just say something? Being hard on crime is OK, but what about children and crime. Is zero tolerance OK for them too? I think children ...

25. a) Don't you think that the class size affects children's ability to learn, (Julia)? If the group is too big there's little time for each person to ask questions or for the teacher to help solve individual problems. (...)

b) At times we do get too much work, don't we, (Peter)? I often have to work all evening to complete my homework. (...)

c) Everyone says we've a lot of opportunities but where are they? I don't really see them. What about you, (Tom)? Do you think we have a lot of opportunities? (...)

d) I think computers are very important and we should be using them in all subjects. Perhaps everyone ought to have a laptop instead of a pen and paper. What do you think, (Mary)? Should school children use more technology in the classroom? (...)

e) I think most of our school rules are fair and sensible. What's your opinion, (Lukas)? Are there any rules which you don't find fair?

f) We have quite a good social life outside of the classroom in our school, don't you think so, (Linda)? What about all the discos, films and other things that happen during the year? They're really good, aren't they?

26. Demonstrating is often the only way to show people how strong opinions are. Is there anything that you'd feel so strongly about, (Jane), that you'd join a public demonstration?

Have you ever seen a demonstration, (John)? Or been involved in one? Would you ever go on one?

I sometimes think that people demonstrate without really understanding what they're demonstrating about. What do you think, (Sally)? Do you believe all demonstrators know why they are demonstrating?

I really don't understand why people demonstrate, it never achieves anything – don't you agree, (Mike)?

If you won't stand up and voice your opinions, then you shouldn't moan about things. I'm right, aren't I, (Karen)? You were saying something like this, yesterday – about the people who like to complain but who won't do anything to alter things.

27. a) I believe young people today are much more aware of the world around them and grow up much faster than a few generations ago. But our rights are those of thirty or forty years ago. I would like to see people at eighteen being treated as adults by the law and independent from parents. Do you feel the same, (Karen)? Don't you want to be an adult at eighteen?

b) The Aborigines have been treated badly but at least some action is now taken to make things better. This situation happens all over the world especially where one country has taken over another. Look at the Inuit or what happened in New Zealand. How would you feel, (Harry,) if you were a young Maori today? Would you be happy with life?

c) In my opinion it's not just the individual we should be looking at, it's also other people. Parents are responsible for their children, aren't they? If parents overfeed their kids then they have no chance, do they? If you're ten and weigh 50 kilos there's not a lot you can do about it, is there? I'm right, aren't I, (Jenny)?

d) There's not enough action taken to stamp out smoking. The problem is that governments like the money they get from the tax, so they never take a hard stand and they're scared of creating unemployment in the tobacco industry. My opinion is that cigarettes should cost about double what they are now and smokers should have to pay for a special health insurance. I'm sure these two simple things would reduce smoking overnight and stop young people starting. (Sue), you smoke, what would you do if your cigarettes suddenly cost ten or fifteen euros a packet?

28.

theme	*Prince of Wales*
main points	*future king / boring wait / Charles very active / projects*
comments	*sad life / difficult / can't leave / Charles successful - made his own job and life*
opinions	*old-fashioned attitude / eldest child should be heir / monarch should be able to abdicate*
focus	*Charles's work / eldest son and not child / out-dated system / abdication*
wider thinking	*people live longer - heir might never be king / what do the people want? / is the monarchy needed? / role of royal family*
experiences	*friends who have to take over parents' businesses*
general knowledge	*British royal family / monarchy*
questions	*e.g. How would you feel if you knew your future was already planned out by someone else?*

29. a)

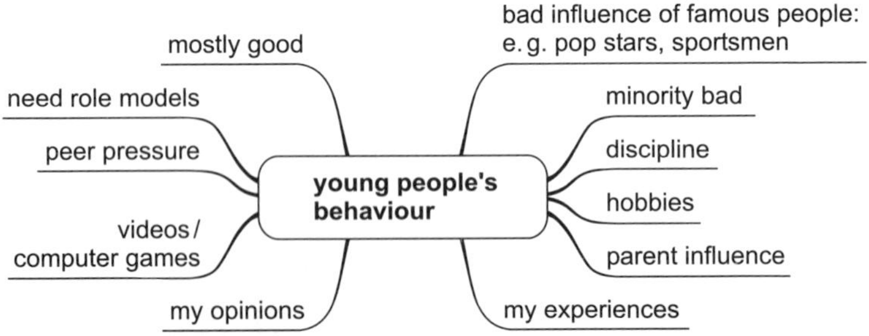

b) *a typical weekend:* sport / hobbies / TV / homework / helping at home / friends / depends upon the weather / out on Friday and Saturday night: disco, cinema …

c) *advertising and sport:* good business / influence of famous people / too much money / effective / different forms / peer pressure result / sponsorship / my experiences / my opinions …

d) *expanding the European Union:* why? / advantages for poor countries, disadvantages for old Europe / EU too big / where? / different cultures / financial costs / employment in new areas, unemployment in old areas / incentives and unfair competition / economic reasons / people's opinions / my opinions / my experiences …

e) *the future of institutions, such as the British Commonwealth or the UN:* examples / efficiency / too bureaucratic / effectiveness / roles, functions / old-fashioned / their image / my experiences / my opinions …

31. a)

poverty	Armut
wealth	Reichtum
struggle	Kampf
(to be) formed	gegründet
economy	Wirtschaft
was booming	boomte
economic growth	Wirtschaftswachstum
available	verfügbar
asylum seekers	Asyl Suchende
community	Gemeinschaft

b)

theme	*the Irish Republic: past, growth, problems*
main points	*poverty to wealth / rapid growth / problems of new money / changing country*
comments	*too much too fast? / money is changing a whole society / new problems arising, racism / changing into a multicultural society / …*
opinions	*sad that a culture is disappearing / good that Ireland is growing / good that young people now want to stay / growth of racism is a shame / …*
focus	*the effects of sudden wealth / attitudes of young people / …*
wider thinking	*are other European countries going to have same problems? / as poor countries get help and do better, do developed countries get worse? / …*
experiences	*visiting poorer countries*
general knowledge	*Ireland*
questions	*e.g. Don't you think too many people like to live in the past and not accept that changes are better?*

c)

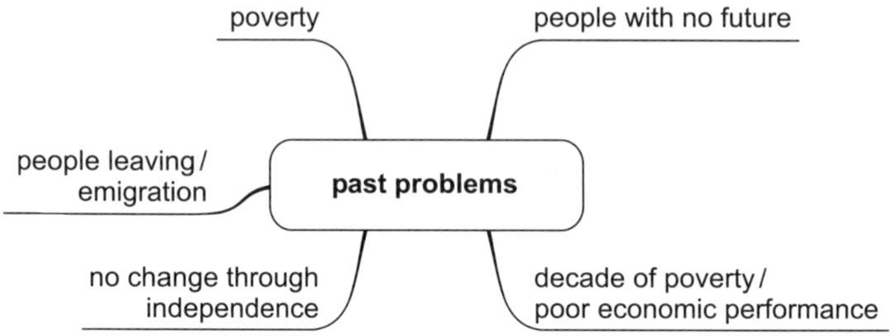

the worries of the Irish: traffic congestion / house prices / immigration / too much, too fast / multicultural society developing / racism / asylum seekers / young people / money-minded people / losing its character and identity …

having new money: sudden change / people's expectations / people lose values / people change / brings new problems / not always good / people's frustrations …

racism: why? / immigration / multicultural society developing / problems / asylum seekers / educate people to accept change / answers to problem? …

young people: changing attitudes / alcohol / too much money / futures? / changing values / staying in Ireland / well-paid, part-time jobs / buying homes …

d)

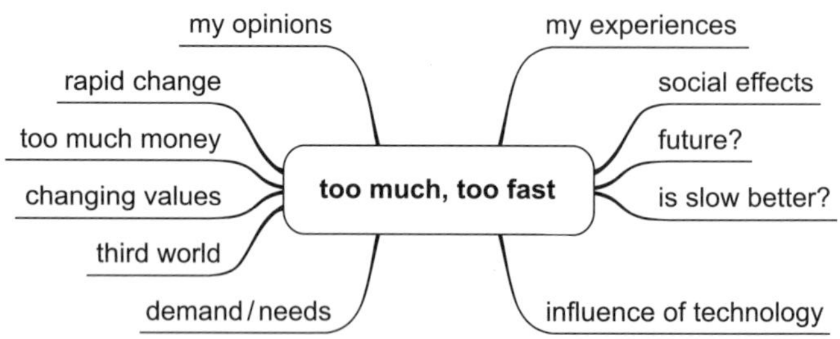

developing countries: help needed / unstable regions, corruption / avoid mistakes / new problems / slow progress better? / costs / who pays? / development leads to developed countries' unemployment / open new markets and destroy old ones / my opinions / my experiences …

asylum seekers: problems / numbers / definitions / reasons / how to stop it / advantages? / government role, policy / my opinions / my experiences …

old ways and traditions versus modern living: cultural clashes / value of tradition / global village / romanticising past / changing attitudes / always social change / old people like old ways / old ways not necessarily good ways / my opinions / my experiences …

integrated societies: idealistic / different cultures / pick and mix culture / understanding each other / problems / globalisation / not new, look at British Isles: Celts, Danes, Normans … / prejudices / my opinions / my experiences …

32. a)

b)

theme	London / congestion / transport methods
main points	no congestion / commuters / different transport methods / rich and showing off / being practical / …
comments	surprising lack of traffic / central London / crowds of people / the rich showing off / congestion charges working? / …
opinions	congestion charges work / people with money still enter / commuters use different forms of transport / need for some people to show off / …
focus	congestion charges / inner-city traffic problems / daily life in cities / …

wider thinking	the environment and pollution / rich and famous / different lifestyles / the need to be seen / ...
experiences	visits to other cities / park and ride systems / problems in my own area / ...
general knowledge	congestion charges in London / motorway charges / American toll lanes and car sharing / ...
questions	e.g. Would you want to be driven around in a stretched limousine and have everyone stare at you?

c) *What do I know about London?* (busy, capital, congestion, congestion charge, many people, many visitors, business centre …)

Why are there so few vehicles? (it's midday – there should be more, crossroads or traffic lights, has congestion charge worked? …)

Where is Piccadilly Circus? (central London, very busy area, London landmark, why is it so empty of cars? …)

Why is the man on a bike? (collapsible bike, a commuter, avoiding congestion charge, a city employee, is it dangerous in London? easier to get about London? …)

What does the picture show? (different ways to travel, different types of people: rich and famous, impractical car, outwardly displaying wealth: bike – practical and down to earth, very little reaction to large car, a normal scene in London? …)

What are the people doing? (sightseeing, visiting, …)

d)

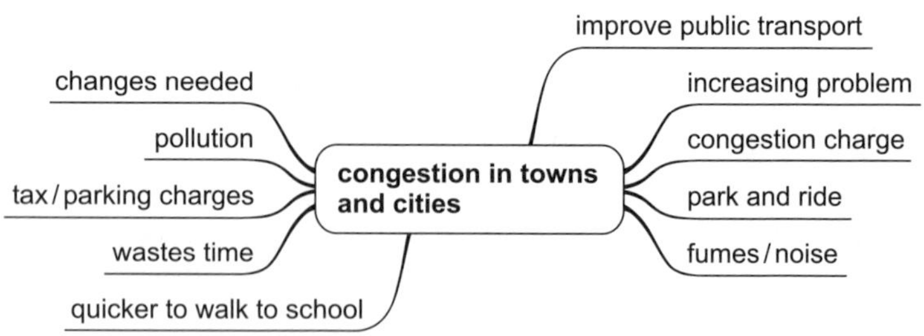

poverty and wealth: big difference today / differences between countries / help for poor / new money / class is not money / credit culture / money orientated society / see differences in school / my experiences / my opinions …

commuting: length of time / why? / how? / cost / by public services or car? / pollution / relaxing or stressful / would I do it? / my opinions / my experiences (e.g. parents) …

cars and the environment: environmentally friendly fuels / pollution / congestion / convenience / educate about use / necessary and unnecessary journeys / parents' attitudes / difference in world use / would I drive a lot ? / my choice of car / my opinions / my experiences

33. a)

b)

theme	*historic moment - downfall of the Wall / graffiti*
main points	*remembering a historic occasion / different forms of graffiti / political freedom / ...*
comments	*keeping the Wall? / the Wall as a gallery for expression / why do people add graffiti? / what should remain? / tourism / ...*
opinions	*graffiti looks bad / vandalism / should keep historic things / social history is important / ...*
focus	*the importance of history / keeping some reminders of the past / the social reasons for graffiti / freedom of expression / ...*

wider thinking	*romanticising the past / what is freedom? / other countries under restrictions / different ways of seeing the world / ...*
experiences	*parents' experiences / graffiti in my environment / frustration / ...*
general knowledge	*November 89 - today's attitudes / actions of young people*
questions	*e.g. How free is the freedom of expression in our society?*

c)

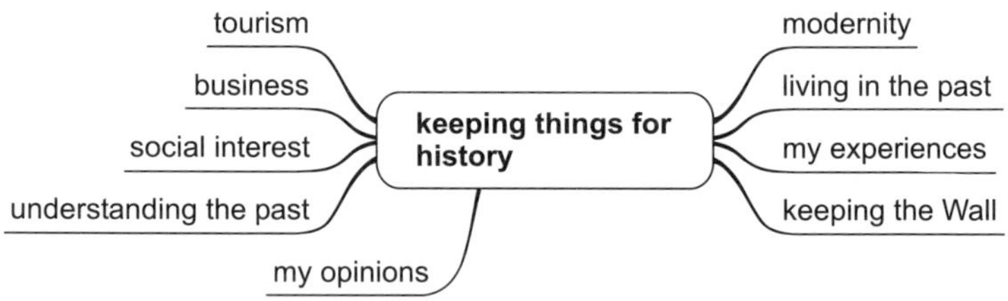

graffiti or freedom to express oneself: vandalism / visual effects / areas look bad, poor and rough / why destroy things? / mentality / expression can be different / needn't deface (other people's property) / done by a minority / how to stop it? / graffiti as art form / my opinions / my experiences …

political statements through the arts: art, music, film, cartoons / e.g. Picasso's Guernica / political songs / e.g. Michael More – Bowling for Columbine / freedom of expression / political censorship / my opinions / my experiences …

tourist attractions: business, jobs, money / too many, too few / tourism brings environmental problems / spoil areas / cultural, scientific, social history, scenic / romanticising the past / hands-on attractions / educational / understanding the past / my experiences / my opinions …

34.

theme	*pupil selection by schools*
main points	*selection not by ability but by social background / good schools have too many applicants / parent not child acceptability / working-class parents disadvantaged / ...*

comments	is selection fair? / discrimination and abuse of system? / leads to good and bad schools / can weaker schools ever improve? / ...
opinions	academic selection is OK / selection through social class is wrong / schools should be able to refuse badly behaved pupils / danger of creating private schools through the backdoor / ...
focus	why selection is happening and how? / ...
wider thinking	other selection processes / fairness of society / equal rights / discrimination / ...
experiences	friends discriminated against because of how they look / ...
general knowledge	selection processes in Britain / private and state schools / problems in education / ...
questions	e.g. Is it right that children's futures are decided by how their parents look or what job they do?

d) the multicultural classroom / social segregation

e) **schools selecting their pupils**

no

- children's education not parent's image
- everyone should have same opportunities
- how do you select?
- who selects?
- some school has to take the less desirable pupils
- non-academic selection

yes

- to maintain standards
- to allow those who want to be educated the chance to do so without disruptive children
- at interviews any parent can make an effort to look nice
- if a school is full, then a selection must be made
- supportive parents are essential for a good school

appearances count: how others see you / fashion / jobs and clothes / peer pressure / money factor / the person is important, not the appearance / cost of dressing correctly / my opinions / my experiences …

problem pupils: school's policies / disruption / damage the learning of others / reduce opportunities in the classroom / minority / home backgrounds / social problems / understand or punish? / separate and isolate? / repeat offenders / my opinions / my experiences …

measuring success: exam results only / grades only / what is success? / different ability levels / academic and non-academic success / positive marking or negative marking / should schools compete? / dangers and advantages of school league tables / my opinions / my experiences …

education and money: cost of education / free education / money for books and visits, etc. / should costs be limited? / poor children feel uncomfortable when parents cannot afford things / parental background and effects / unequal opportunities / schools' expectations, e. g. computers / my opinions / my experiences …

the multicultural classroom: increasingly more common / advantages / cultural diversity / alternative viewpoints and experiences / understanding other cultures / problems of language, beliefs, customs / levels and abilities / more teachers of foreign backgrounds needed / need to train for multicultural classroom teaching / my opinions / my experiences …

social segregation: segregated by money, culture, background / social isolation / outcast / bullying / mobbing / integration / religion / discrimination / equal opportunities? / expectations / my opinions / my experiences …

35. a)

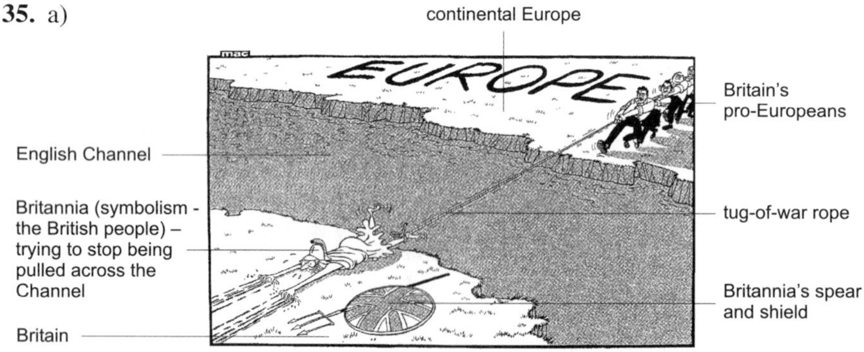

'Nearly there ...wait for it ...wait for it'

b)

theme	*Britain and Europe / Britons not willing to join Europe*
main points	*anti-European feeling / Britons don't want to be part of Europe / Labour party taking a country into Europe which doesn't want to be there / ...*
comments	*why is there anti-European feeling? / is Britain special because of being an island? / politicians acting against what people want / ...*
opinions	*people should be asked to vote on European issues / people scared of losing identity / politicians should listen to the people they represent / ...*
focus	*anti-European feelings / identities / ...*
wider thinking	*many large groups don't work / the need for working together / English as the world's language / ...*
experiences	*euro and effects / holidaying in Europe / parents' fears and experiences / ...*
general knowledge	*how EU developed / planned expansions / economics / ...*
questions	*e.g. Don't you see the benefits of a larger Europe?*

c)

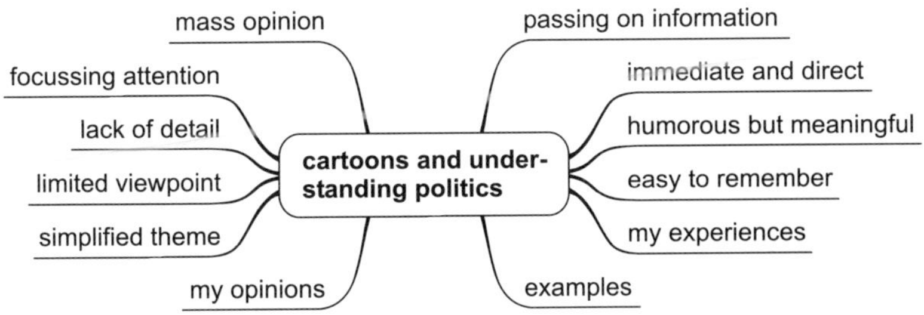

freedom of speech and expression: ways of expression / censorship / benefit of democracy / freedom with limitations / is the West free? / a point to fight for? / my opinions / my experiences …

politicians and the people: do they represent the people? / self-interest / image / trust / role models / should they do what the majority want? / keep promises? / speak truthfully? / disillusionment / my opinions / my experiences …

the European Union: too big / people don't want it / loss of independence / trade advantages / social advantages / mobility of workers / euro / a European language – English? / where does enlargement stop? / inequality in the EU / advantages and disadvantage of enlarging into weaker economies / my opinions / my experiences …

d) *cartoons and understanding politics:*
- Don't you agree, (Mike), that cartoons help you to see the problems in politics clearer?
- Do you look at the cartoons in the paper, (Jana)?

freedom of speech and expression:
- We might have freedom of speech but we can't use it freely. What do you think, (Tom)?
- (Karen), you listen to weird music a lot, don't you ever think about the lyrics? You know, what are they saying, what's the message?

politicians and the people:
- Don't you get angry, (David), when politicians say one thing one day and then do something else the next?
- I feel I can't trust politicians anymore. Does anyone else feel this way? What about you, (Tina)?

the European Union:
- I don't want to lose my identity and be a European. And you, (Maria)? Do you want to have a European nationality?
- Shouldn't we just accept that English will be the language of Europe and start using it now and forget about our own? I think German will be as useful as Gaelic, eventually. What's your opinion, (Henry)?

36. b)

theme	car technology
main points	car that controls itself in traffic by adjusting speeds, keeping distances and by stopping
comments	safer / high-tech cars / dependency on technology / …
opinions	safety is always good / is the driver becoming unnecessary? / does technology give a false safety feel? /should all safety things be standard and not optional? / …
focus	too much technology / passive or active in the driving seat
wider thinking	what happens when technology fails? / driverless cars? / controlling congestion / …
experiences	father's car full of technology that is never used / …

general knowledge	*technology that is on the market / how our dependency on technology is increasing / ...*
questions	*e.g. Is technology making people unnecessary? For example, driving a car involves skills, but technology is reducing those that are required. What's your opinion?*

c) knowing how to and needing / a new throw-away generation

d)

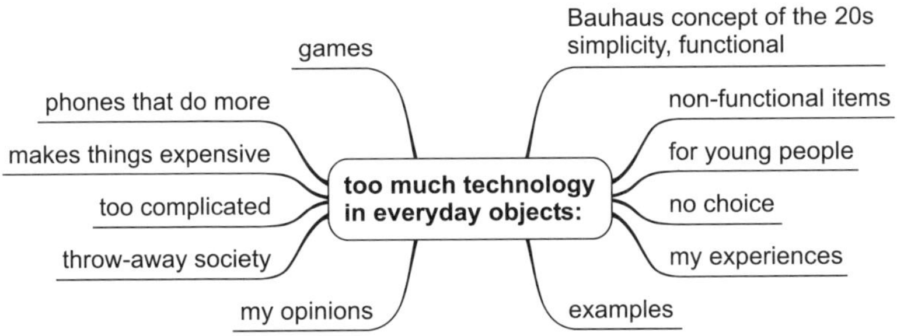

living in a technological world: necessary to use technology / makes life easier / busier / more hectic / reduces social communications / globalisation / my opinions / my experiences …

parents and technology – a generation gap?: limited parental know-how / children know more / parents ask children for help / role reversals / parents insecure / brings families together / similar interests / my opinions / my experiences …

technology and social breakdown: lack of real communications / people forget how to talk to each other / people live apart / not near friends / no need to know about the neighbours / breakdown in community life / friends are selected / new friends hard to make / loneliness without being alone / my opinions / my experiences …

knowing how to and needing: what is necessary? / advances are good / does every new concept need to be sold? / developments lead to others / bigger, newer, quicker generation / is technological revolution good or bad? / my opinions / my experiences …

a new throw-away generation: technology quickly outdated / encouraged to throw away / repairs cost more than new equipment / lives full of things no one needs or wants / gimmick sales for young people / addiction to technology / pollution and environmental problems from manufacturing and throwing away / my opinions / my experiences …

37. a)

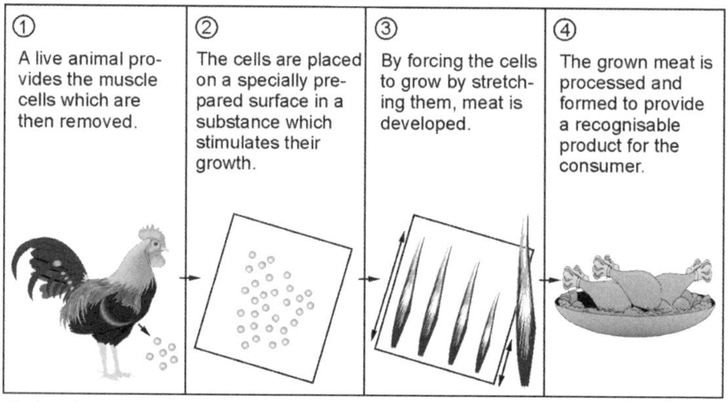

① showing origin of cells: chicken (this could be any animal)
② showing how the cells are prepared: on special sheets and individually laid out
③ cells made bigger to make meat
④ meat is made into a product to sell: for, example chicken legs
clear stages in the process identified
doesn't show: mass production methods / health risks / time for cell growth / taste …

b)

theme	*cloning meat*
main points	*easy to clone meat and make it into anything people want*
comments	*how is this done? / can one sell it? / ...*
opinions	*could help food problem in Third World / do we know what we eat? / is this real meat? / health risks? / do not like the idea / playing with nature / is this really a good idea? / no real benefit / ...*
focus	*the problem of a vegetarian / is this meat? / should it be sold as meat? / ...*
wider thinking	*many food problems in recent years, isn't this another danger? / playing with nature / terrorism and the food chain / ...*
experiences	*being a vegetarian / ...*
general knowledge	*cloning / ...*
questions	*e.g. You eat a sausage now not knowing what goes into it - all the rubbish. Isn't this just the same?*

c) changes in agriculture / technology in the food industry

d) 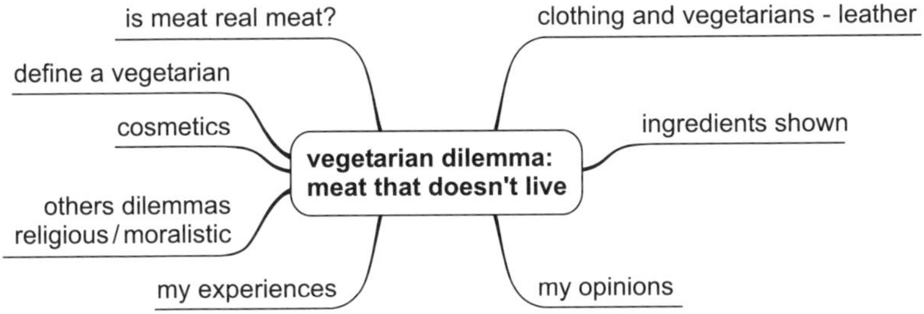

the food we eat: origins / fresh? / chemicals / food miles / over-production / resources / everything's available / supermarket influences / at other people's expense / poverty and starvation / waste / my opinions / my experiences …

cloning:
advantages: medical / cures / spare part transplants /…
disadvantages: playing God / abuse / dangers / how long before a human clone? … / my opinions / …

providing for the Third World: help but education better / teach how to do things / balancing western food consumption with third-world starvation / help and food is just a plane journey away / costs / developed countries' waste / my opinions / my experiences …

changes in agriculture: was labour intensive / mechanical / effects of government help / globalisation / transport advances / food economics / influence of supermarkets / satisfying demands / local produce / my opinions / my experiences …

technology in the food industry:
advantages: quick / effective / wide choice / long-lasting food / anything anytime
disadvantages: chemicals / why have so much choice? / are products all year round necessary? / my opinions / my experiences …

e) *vegetarian dilemma: meat that doesn't live:*
- Vegetarians may care about what they eat but not how the leather for their shoes or the fat in cosmetics came about. What's your opinion?
- I think everyone has the right to eat what they want. I object to vegetarians who try to make you feel bad when you eat meat, don't you agree?

the food we eat:

– Wouldn't it be a good idea to have food with big labels on – 'made in a lab' – 'full of fat' – that sort of thing? I'm right aren't I?
– I'm not sure I really want to know what I'm eating. Does anyone else feel the same? Can you imagine what goes into a sausage?

cloning:

– How would you feel if you were a clone – wouldn't you feel strange?
– Aren't we in danger of having a society that doesn't know who it's related too? With sperm and egg donors, for example, you might marry your brother or sister. Have you ever though about this, (Anne)?

providing for the Third World:

– We could all do more for the Third World, couldn't we?
– Come on, (Mike) tell me how much food you throw away every day?

changes in agriculture:

– Shouldn't supermarkets have to say where their products come from?
– I would like to say, 'Isn't it time to return to real products made by nature?' but that's impossible. What's the alternative then? To eat chemicals?

technology in the food industry:

– Isn't is stupid that often the food we eat has been flown half way around the world before we eat it?
– (Jenny), don't you think it's great that, today, you can have whatever you want at any time?

▶ Aufgaben im Stil der mündlichen Prüfung

Brandenburg – Mündliche Gruppenprüfung
Aufgabe 1: ***The role of the media – advertising***

Read the text and answer the questions.

Advertising strategies

The idea of advertising is not to sell but to get people to buy. If you think about this, then you can see that the advertising world is a very clever place. There are many different types of advertising strategies. In newspapers the adverts are often simple – this offer or that offer, for example. Television adverts, though, can be more fun, and effective, they sell lifestyles, for example a pair of jeans suddenly makes you cool and attractive. There are even prizes given for the best TV adverts – the Oscars of the advertising world. And don't forget those annoying songs or phrases which, although they really are annoying, keep you remembering the product.

But there are also other types of advertising. One is called 'product placement', that means, for example, James Bond driving the latest Aston Martin which then sells Aston Martins. This works just as much with normal products, too, for example BWMs in German detective series. This way of advertising is not just used for cars, however, it includes all types of consumer products and services, such as drinks and chocolates or airlines and banks.

Sponsorship is another form of advertising. Sportsmen with labels such as Nike or Adidas over their clothes make people turn to these shelves in the sport shops. But this type of advertising does not end there. The customer buys something with the company's logo on it and then walks about with it. This is now free advertising for the company. *247 words*

Assignments

1. Talk about different forms of advertising. What do you know about them and the methods used? How successful do you think they are?
   (text information / types: newspapers, television … / indirect or direct … / targeted customers / …)

2. What is your personal reaction to advertisements? Talk about the best advert that you have seen.
   (on TV / in magazines / product placement / …)

3. Do we live in a world that is too commercialised?
   (pressure to buy / fashion / trends / Christmas / …)

Group discussion

1. What do you think about product placement? Should it be allowed in schools? *(what is product placement? / advantages and disadvantages / if educational, OK – for example banks, driving schools / ...)*

2. Fashion, trends and advertising. What influence do they have on young people?
(explain what each means / examples: clothes, hair styles ... / peer pressure / role models ...)

3. Imagine you are the executives of a new airline which flies from Germany's major airports to other European cities. How would you advertise your company and where?
(in which way would you try to be different in a competitive world? – comfort, young people / what action are you going to take to make your company a success? – service, price / ...)

Lösungsvorschläge

Assignments

1. There are many different forms of adverting that I know about and are mentioned in the text. The most common types are the ones you see in newspapers and on TV but advertising is a very wide area. An example, however, of indirect advertising is something called product placement. This is where a product is put or used in a very prominent place and people see it all the time. Another form of advertising is sponsorship, for example footballers wearing the logos of companies. Wearing brand names is not just limited to sportspeople, though. We all do it. My friends and I often wear T-shirts, for example with Adidas or some other brand written on them. Customers wearing a firm's logo is really free advertising for the firm. The methods of advertising are many from large billboard posters to short ads at the cinema, they can also be seen on buses, cars and plastic bags. Not only is there indirect and direct advertising there are also different ways of advertising, for example by being serious or humorous, by cartoons or real actors. Potential customers are often targeted, for example the young, because they have money to spend on certain products. Advertising is very successful and often we are 'brainwashed' into buying something without even being aware of what is happening. Just think of how many products and brand names you know. (...)

2. I don't mind advertisements on TV but I dislike programmes being frequently interrupted. Some ads on TV are fun but sadly not too many of them. I particularly like the adverts that involve something more than just someone telling you to buy something. I enjoy the ones that are entertaining and which are sometimes like short films. Recently I particularly liked an ad for Citroen cars where the car suddenly transforms itself into a techno-dancing robot and then transforms itself back into the car again at the end. One of my big hates, though, is when I buy a magazine with more adverts than articles in it. This sometimes occurs. Once I counted forty full-page adverts in a magazine with only fifty-two pages; and then the other pages were taken up with things like the contents' list, large photos and large headings. Product placement is OK and not, it really depends on what and where. If I watch a film full of BMWs, I don't go and tell my parents they need to buy a BMW. But I'm sure I am influenced in some way by this method. Of course the world is full of posters, they're everywhere. I usually read them mainly because I want to see if there's anything to do at the weekend, for example. (...)

3. I guess we do live in a commercialised world. To be honest I don't really know if it's too bad. Sometimes things annoy me but not as much as they

annoy my parents. There's a lot of pressure to buy certain things because school friends have them. If you don't, then you are often laughed at. But fashion changes quickly with trends being created rather than being developed. My parents' fashions lasted many years and they developed slowly from one thing to another. Today, it always appears to me that as soon as one type of fashion style is on the market another is quickly created and marketed so that young people will have to buy something new again very quickly afterwards. My parents think that Christmas is too early in the shops. They always complain when they see the first sights of Christmas in October. I don't really care because I don't do any Christmas shopping until very late anyway. I've read in a newspaper that many people, however, spend more than they have and that people are encouraged to go into debt. I hope I won't become one of those people, but it is easy to see why and how this happens. Sometimes, though, I wonder why there is so much choice. When I buy something, the choice is usually very wide. (...)

Group discussion

1. what is product placement? – having a company's product or image in a very public place such as a theatre, or a cinema / advantages – company sells and workers keep jobs, can bring money to something without money, can organise competitions ... / disadvantages – who wants to watch a theatre play with a beefburger on stage, when advertising and the situation have no connection it spoils the real atmosphere / in schools it may be OK if educational – e. g. banks, driving schools, can also bring money into school for equipment or books / your experiences / your opinions / ...

2. explain what each means / examples – clothes, hair styles, music, shoes, sport equipment, tattoos, piercing / peer pressure / role models such as pop stars / some fashions or trends are forever such as tattoos / young people influenced through image / role models should see their responsibility / young people like having individuality but also being identified with a group / your experiences / your opinions /...

3. to be different in a competitive world / comfort / target age groups e. g. young people / fly at good times / offer extra things, e. g. free car parking / actions for success? – service, price, customer care, quality food / ... advertise on TV, in magazines, stickers, word of mouth, T-shirts and other products / examples of good practice / your experiences / your opinions / ...

Brandenburg – Mündliche Gruppenprüfung
Aufgabe 2: ***Environment and health care***

Look at the diagram and answer the questions.

Food that moves

Other facts:

- In America every kilogram of food has on average travelled 3,500 kilometres before going onto the dinner table.
- Britain imports 430,000 tonnes of butter every year from the EU and exports 470,000 tonnes to the same areas.
- A German yoghurt including the container travels on average 8,000 kilometres before getting to a shop.

Assignments

1. Talk about the information. How do you react to food being moved around the world, especially when things can be got nearer to where you live?
   (what is the subject? / details given / opinions / …)

2. Only the price counts. Should we care where food and consumer products come from?
   (environment / how things are grown / opinion / experiences / …)

3. Talk about the way people shop.
   (generation differences / small shops / Internet / superstores / …)

Group discussion

1. BSE, hormones, chemicals, cloning: What is the future of food?
   (all the problems of food technology, why and what can be done – how do you expect the future to be in 10 or 20 years' time? – a return to people growing their own? / …)

2. Are we educated enough to keep us healthy?
   (educating about good and bad food / compulsory exercise / smoking / leading by example / …)

3. Global responsibility: who cares and who should?
   (pollution from transport, overeating and famine … / young people / governments / …)

Lösungsvorschläge

Assignments

1. The illustration and the few notes that are with it show how food often travels a very long way before it arrives at a dinner table. I was quite shocked at the distances which this involves. I wonder why, for example, carrots need to be flown over 9500 kilometres to end up in Britain. I really can't imagine that doing this is cheaper than buying the vegetable in Britain. What I find terrible, though, is the amount transporting food around the world costs in other terms, for example the pollution caused. It does show the effects of globalisation, however, and how efficient transport is today.
   What worries me, though, is that I'm sure supermarkets must force prices down by buying such large amounts from poorer areas. I hope that these firms deal fairly with these producers, but I doubt it. Sadly, no one really cares where their food comes from so long as it's cheap. Perhaps we should. What I really don't understand is why products cannot be grown nearer the markets. I don't really see how a few hundred kilos of beef flown half way around the world can be cheaper than local meat. (…)

2. Unfortunately, I think only the price really does count. Everyone says they care but no one is prepared to pay more for their caring. When I take time to think about the situation, I find that we abuse the environment a lot simply by the food we eat. We create pollution by moving it from one place to another and this is even worse when things are flown. To have many things all year round a large amount of water for the plants is often required. And because we want our food products to be healthy-looking, farmers pour chemicals on the land damaging eco-systems.
   But it is not just the food industry where we should be aware of the origins of produce. It's also important to know where everything comes from. Many cheaply made clothes, for example, are the result of people working in very poor conditions often involving child labour in third-world countries. Again, we only think about how much things cost. It would be nice to see companies having to display in large letters where the country of origin is. Better still would be a code of conduct for businesses whereby those companies that follow it are awarded a noticeable award. (…)

3. My grandparents often talk about how they used to always go to small corner shops and family-owned ones in the town centre. They enjoyed this way of shopping and knew that what they bought was fresh – or as fresh as it could be in those days. The things they bought were usually locally grown, too. My parents, though, grew up with supermarkets and so they prefer them. These

large out-of-town stores offer more choice and now people expect a large choice everywhere. But people still want cheap products. The problem with supermarkets or large stores is that small shops can't compete. As a result the small stores of my grandma's time have all gone out of business. Today, my generation has the Internet. And Internet shopping is very easy. I'm sure in a few years' time shopping over the Internet will also put many people out of business. My parents already book all our holidays over the Internet – we used to go to a travel agent's, but no more. Probably one of the biggest on-line stores is Amazon. To be honest, I know very few people who do not use this company.

In spite of the Internet I still like looking at things in the shops and I think most people do, too. I know that often my parents look for what they want in the shops and then go home and look for it on the Internet and see if there's a price difference. (…)

Group discussion

1. the problems of food technology / why and what can be done / the future in 10 or 20 years' time? / a return to people growing their own products / do people care? / are people willing to change? / is cloning the way to stop starvation and famine? / if you play with nature what happens? / your experiences / your opinions / …

2. educating about good and bad food / healthy eating / diets / compulsory exercise in schools / smoking – evidence that words don't matter, need strong action instead / non-smoking areas / leading by example – doctors, teachers, role models / education is not just schools – government should educate too, by adverts or forcefully by taxes and other actions / your experiences / your opinions / …

3. pollution from transport / overeating / famine / wars / … / young people are the future – responsible / governments should make people do things / governments should force global offenders to stop and change / everyone should take more responsibility, for example with rubbish, recycling, water wastage / problems of tourism / …

Brandenburg – Mündliche Gruppenprüfung
Aufgabe 3: *Past, present, future – New Zealand*

Read the interview and answer the questions.

Talking about New Zealand

I seldom hear anything about New Zealand. What's it like, Andrew?
It's isolated. We're a country in the middle of nowhere. From Europe, we're on the other side of the globe. A lot of people do know things about it, though, they've heard about the Maoris and that New Zealand is two islands, and, of course, the sheep. You may also know of films that have been made there. *Babe* was one – a story about a pig which talked – and, of course, *Lord of the Rings* was filmed there.

What don't we know about New Zealand, then?
We're a green country and don't like nuclear weapons or nuclear power. We don't allow American ships that are carrying nuclear weapons or are powered by nuclear energy, into our waters. The Americans, of course, don't like that.

Do New Zealanders learn foreign languages?
No, not really. I learnt a little French and Japanese at school but because we live on an island in the middle of nowhere languages aren't encouraged. But travelling around the world I see how important languages are and I wish I'd learnt one well at school.

What's the weather like?
Wet!

Why did you leave New Zealand?
New Zealand is very isolated and young people, like myself, need to see what is happening in the rest of the world. So, often we just travel around for a few years and meet other people and see other places. I've been away from home, now, for three years.

What have you gained from travelling?
I've seen and experienced a lot of things. I've also had the opportunity to do things I'd not have done at home. I think I've got a different view of politics now, too, and I'm more aware of other people. At home people just see themselves.

Annotations: isolated – *abgelegen;* in the middle of nowhere – *am Ende der Welt;* waters – *Gewässer;* (to be) aware – *bewusst (sein)*

Assignments

1. What does Andrew tell you about New Zealand? Is this different to how you saw New Zealand and what you knew about it before reading the interview? *(text details / what do you know about New Zealand? / Maoris / where is it? / have you seen any films about it? / read any books? / have you seen any of the films mentioned? / …)*
2. What are the advantages and disadvantages of travel? *(think about what Andrew says / lonely / miss friends / money / need to be older / …)*
3. If you could go anywhere in the world, where would you go? *(why and for how long? / what would you hope to achieve? / how would you travel? / …)*

Group discussion

1. Most of us don't know how other people live. Should we? *(need to understand cultures / see how lucky we are / understand the world and other people's ways of life / …)*
2. If you really want to do something, you'll do it. Talk about this. *(often people say they want to do something but won't try to do it / excuses rather than trying / working to be the best – look at sportsmen, pop stars and actors / …)*
3. How important is it for young people to escape their own environment and broaden their horizons – this may include travel? *(need to explore / discover things / be independent / …)*

Lösungsvorschläge

Assignments

1. Andrew explains how isolated New Zealand is. When you look at a map it always seems to be just off the coast of Australia but this is untrue. It's actually a long way from anywhere. New Zealand is made up of two islands and it's a large sheep farming area. It has had a few famous films made there as well. The one that probably everyone my age knows is Lord of the Rings, but I remember watching Babe when I was younger. What I didn't know was that New Zealand is a green country and it's strongly anti-nuclear.
   Andrew explains how language learning is not encouraged and I can understand now why not. If there is no need to use a language, then why learn it? Since English is a world language we have to speak it but which language should New Zealanders learn? I never thought of New Zealand as being wet, either, but if Andrew describes it in this simple way it must mean it's very wet! I was surprised to hear that so many young people leave and travel. Again, now someone has said this, I can understand why it happens. In Europe we are so lucky. It is no problem to go to many different countries but New Zealanders have little choice, if any. (...)

2. For me, the biggest advantage of travel is that is gives you the sense of adventure and independence. I enjoy going to different countries and when I am older I hope to see more. I think it's important to see the world, meet new people and see how other people and countries work. You realise that things don't have to be how they are in your own country. The experience that you gain makes you a better person, I think. You think differently and see things in new ways.
   I'm surprised Andrew never felt lonely, though, and missed his family and friends. I don't know if I would if I travelled but it would certainly be one of the disadvantages of travel which I would expect. I guess you would need a lot of money, too, unless you can work in some places that you come to. At the moment, I would feel a little scared to travel the world by myself but maybe in a few years' time that will change. I think a great disadvantage for me would be not having someone else by my side. The other problem with travelling is when to do it. If I start to work, then I would need to stop again so that I could travel. I would certainly not get my job back. This is a great disadvantage while there is high unemployment around. (...)

3. The world is a very big place but I would love to go to China. I want to go there because I think that it is at the start of a period of huge change and I want to see the real China before it all changes. I would like to see all the

sights, of course, like the Great Wall of China and the Terracotta Army. The temples and palaces would also be interesting. But, I would also really want to see how people live, for example in small villages. I think it would be great to be able to stay in a few people's homes to see how Chinese people really are and what they eat. I'm also curious to see what the inside of their houses looks like.

Of course, I would also want to go to see some of the large cities like Beijing or Shanghai. These must be ultra-modern cities but I could imagine that there is a lot of poverty there. Chinese people always give me the impression of being warm and friendly people so I think I would enjoy the country very much. (…)

Group discussion

1. need to understand cultures / see how lucky we are / understand the world and other people's ways of life / understanding customs / respecting each other / knowledge / taking the best pieces of other cultures / globalisation means contact with more cultures / multicultural societies / people working abroad / your experiences / your opinions / …

2. people often say they want to do something but won't try to do it / excuses rather than trying / working to be the best – look at sportsmen, pop stars and actors / being committed / positive attitudes and ways to do things / knowing what you want to do / being selfish / if you don't do things, you can't complain / people's attitudes / your experiences / your opinions / …

3. need to explore / discover things / be independent / can escape home area / if living in a bad area with no future, they can move / important to take charge of one's life / influence of others – family and friends / moving away doesn't mean losing friends / new friends / new experiences / new chances / can start again / in a competitive world it shows you are different / your experiences / your opinions / …

Brandenburg – Mündliche Gruppenprüfung
Aufgabe 4: *Politics and economy*

Read the letter and look at the cartoon, then answer the questions.

The new throw-away society

Dear Sir,

Are we going to be a new throw-away society? If I look at technology today, I think Ireland and the rest of the world are going to have some very big problems in the future.

Last week, two things happened. The first was that my computer stopped working. The person who looks after my computer said that it would be too expensive to repair, at least €200 for the part and then his time. He also said that the computer was six years old and belonged in a museum – I disagreed. The result was that I bought a new computer and threw the old one away. But then my scanner wouldn't work with the new computer software, neither would the printer. I could either install the old software and not use the new computer for what I needed it or buy a new scanner and printer. Of course, everything was thrown away again.

Secondly, my son wanted another mobile phone. He could phone people with his first one but that wasn't 'cool', so he got a new one with which he could take photos, play games, text people and many other things, too. Now that is no longer 'cool', so he's saving his money up to buy another new one that will do even more things than the one he has at the moment. Then he'll throw away the good phone – and in a few months' time it'll all start again.

Where is this big hole in the ground for all this throw-away equipment to go to and where are the endless resources coming from to continue making more?

Kind regards,
Jane Smith

Cartoon

Assignments

1. What is the letter writer complaining about and why? Connect what she says to the cartoon.
   (text information – look at all the details in the cartoon)

2. Talk about balancing the economy, the environment and new technology.
   (opinions / experiences / ideas – recycling … / making people aware / …)

3. Parents once knew more than their children, now children often know more than their parents. Talk about this situation and what it means.
   (using computers and electronic equipment? / is technology too complicated? / bring people together? / parents' attitudes / education / …)

Group discussion

1. Talk about growing up in a technological world.
   (what technology do you have at home – mobile …? / always something new / made the world smaller / more opportunities / …)
2. What are the dangers of modern technology for young people? Who should control the situation?
   (aggression and video games / health problems and computers / responsibilities: parents', governments', manufacturers'… / …)
3. Should the makers of electronic equipment have to take the old ones back and recycle them? What effect would this have?
   (yes / no /save energy / materials / …)

Lösungsvorschläge

Assignments

1. The letter writer is complaining about throwing away things that still work and that modern objects are soon seen as being old. She tells of her experience of her computer. When it broke down it was too expensive to repair and the repairman thought that 6 years old was, anyway, far too old. What she found out, though, was that she couldn't replace only one part of her system and, therefore, she had to also renew parts that worked perfectly well.
   She also writes about her son's attitude. He always wants the most up-to-date mobile phone. She thinks that today's phones are not phones but toys. To some extent she may be right! But she is concerned that we throw things away because we want the newest ones and that today's technology is quickly out-of-date. Of course, if we're always throwing away perfectly good equipment it results in resources being used up and creates unnecessary waste.
   The cartoon shows what the woman is talking about. The scene is typical of any large electronics shop where there are hundreds of mobile phones all capable of doing wonderful things and adverts where, for example, printers are cheaper than the ink they use and where repairs are more expensive than purchasing the product new once again. (…)
2. There are many things to consider, here. There's a very basic need for jobs, for example. People without jobs are often very unhappy and, of course, poor. To provide jobs there needs to be industry. But, on the other hand, no one wants to live in a horrible place that is polluted or wants to damage the world's climate, so therefore, there's also the need to protect our environment.

These three things, though, lead to other things - the need to develop and improve technology, for example, so that industry can progress without harming the environment. In many cases one thing is tightly bound with another.
What is a big concern, I think, is that the third-world countries should not develop in a negative way like the developed world has done, instead they should avoid the mistakes – or be helped to avoid the mistakes. The Industrial Revolution hurt the environment with its polluting factories and carefree attitudes. The question is, will the technological revolution do the same? Manufacturers respond to consumer requirements, so I hope that consumers will start to put pressure on manufacturers to take back old equipment. If not, I hope laws will be passed to do this. I think there should be more public awareness of the balance which is needed between industry, the environment and people. (…)

3. Even when I was younger I always used to ask my mum or my dad for help when I couldn't do something. They were always able to help me and I never really thought much about it. Of course, by helping they were really educating me in everyday things as well. But my parents have grown up in a period where computers were not used in schools and mine, certainly, only use them for work. For them the computer is like a car – they use it and it works, and if it goes wrong it's taken somewhere to be repaired. I understand much more about computers and other electrical equipment because I have grown up with them. Often, therefore, my parents ask me to help them when there's a problem with their computers or other electronic equipment. This is now a sort of role reversal.
If so many people have problems understanding technology, I sometimes wonder if it's too complicated. I also wonder if the infamous generation gap of the 60s and 70s is beginning again through a lack of understanding between parents and children's daily lives. This need for children now to help parents is a peculiar situation and I wonder how frustrating this is for parents and whether there's a certain insecurity on their side because of this. (…)

Group discussion

1. what technology do you have at home – mobile, computer, I-pod …? / always something new / made the world smaller / more opportunities / fast changing / hectic / unfriendly / people don't communicate / rely on computers / children don't play together / wide resources and information at home / have to know about computers / own experience / own opinions / …

2. health worries – mobile phones and cancer / sitting in front of a computer – back problems, eyesight problems, lack of exercise / aggression and video games / your experiences / your opinions / trends and pressure / new mobile phone with a camera, for example, then everyone has to have one / difficult to keep up to date / lack of communication / manufacturer responsibility / government responsibility / school and education / businesses / …

3. yes – they want to sell and change things quickly, must take the responsibility / creation of new industries and jobs / if not taken back then developments in the area don't start / no – people's choice what they buy / save energy by creating new materials / more energy needed to recycle / materials / old things resold to poorer people instead / given to charities and Third World / your experiences / your opinions /…

Brandenburg – Mündliche Gruppenprüfung
Aufgabe 5: *Values and education – looking for employment*

Read the advertisement and answer the questions.

Three Trainee Assistants Required

Northern TV

We are a small television company and have training vacancies for school-leavers in the following areas starting in September: reporting, photography and advertising. We need people who can work as part of a group and by themselves.
We will give you all the training that you need. If you successfully finish our three-year training course we can guarantee you a job.

Trainee reporter: You will need a good level of English and have one foreign language. You will also need to be able to use a computer and be good at talking to people. You have to be able to finish work on time. Send us an example of a report about *young people* together with your application.

Trainee photographer: You will be working with the reporting team. This is a 35-hour-a-week job which may include working evenings and nights. You will have to go on a one-day-a-week course in photography and film making at Northumbria University. Send us *six recent photographs* that you have taken with your application, if you are interested in this vacancy.

Trainee graphic designer: You need to be able to draw, to have ideas and to be able to explain them. You will work with our design team that makes the graphics for our television company. We will teach you how to use the latest computer design programs. Send us your application together with three examples of design work that you have done and an idea for a *Northern TV logo.*

All training periods last three years.

For application forms and further details write to:
Julia Miller, Northern TV, St. Andrew's Lane, Newcastle-upon-Tyne.
Tel: 08561 / 67222 E-mail: miller@northerntv.uk

Annotations: trainee – *Auszubildende/-r;* vacancy – *freie Stelle;* application – *Bewerbung*

Assignments

1. What type of people is the television company looking for and what skills should they have? If you want to apply for the jobs, what do you have to do?
   (text information)

2. What do you think are the good and the bad points of each job? Which of the jobs do you prefer and why?
   (opinions and reasons)

3. For you, what are the most important aspects of a job?
   (explain in detail / money / interesting work / outside / ...)

Group discussion

1. Does school prepare you for work?
   (need for education / Maths, German, English are important / could do more / ...)

2. How do you see the job market for young people?
   (hard / few jobs / need to be mobile / ...)

3. Imagine yourselves as employers, for example Julia Miller at the television company. How would you decide who to give a job to? What questions would you ask someone at an interview and why?
   (think about qualities, skills and exam results, and then the person – appearance, personality ... / ask for introductions / about themselves / find out their interest in the job and their skills / working late and private life / reaction to criticism / ...)

Lösungsvorschläge

Assignments

1. The company is looking for school-leavers who are able to be part of a team and also work independently. They want trainees in three different areas; in news reporting, photography and designing. All the positions include a three-year training course and the company will give a full-time job at the end of this period, if you complete it successfully.
   To be a trainee reporter you are expected to have good English and a foreign language. You also need to be able to use a computer and, of course, you need to be good at talking to people since you'll have to deal with them all the time. It is a demanding job because you have to work to time limits. Reports would have to be finished so that they can be in the programmes at the right time. You need to complete an application form and give an example of your writing ability by producing a report about young people,
   To be a trainee photographer you need to be able to work with other people and be flexible. You will often be needed when something happens, therefore you mustn't mind working nights or evenings if necessary. The company will send you on a special training course at a local university for one day per week so that you learn more about photography and film-making. You have to fill in an application form and enclose with it six recent photos that you have taken.
   The final position is for a trainee graphic designer. Of course, for this job you have to be creative and good at drawing. But you need to have ideas and to be able to talk about ideas and explain them. There's a lot of teamwork involved in this job and much of the work will involve computers, which you will be trained to use. With your application form you must include examples of your artwork by sending in three designs you have done and a suggestion for the company's logo. (…)

2. No matter what job you would like there are always good and bad sides to it. I see these aspects of the jobs in the following way. As a reporter you have to deal with all sorts of people which may be very interesting. I'll also be working independently and can use my English. All these points I find good. What I think is not so good is that the job requires good English and I'm not sure my English is up to this level. I worry that I may not like the people I have to talk to and working to a time limit is stressful. I'm not too good at that in school!
   As a photographer, I like the idea of teamwork and work which is flexible. It's also a great advantage to be sent on a training course because if I decide later I don't like the company I have got a good training in a certain area. The bad

side is that I'm not independent and I've got to do what is wanted. Also, because the working times are not really fixed, and can include evenings and nights, this will affect my social life.
Being a designer sounds interesting and this is the job I would prefer. What would be good is that I could use my own ideas and be creative. The job would also allow me to be, on the one hand, independent but, on the other, allow me to be a member of a team. There is a real chance for my ideas to be used, too. Training with design programs is also given, which I think is very important and something which would be useful if I ever decided to leave. What I think will be difficult is always having to have ideas and teamwork also means working on other people's ideas. (…)

3. At the moment there are two sets of important things for me about work. At the very end of all my wishes and dreams is the fact that I do actually get a job and that, today, is not as easy at it sounds. But I would like to talk about this topic in an idealistic way.
   What's very important, for me, is that I enjoy what I'm doing. I would hate to go to work every day knowing that I wasn't going to enjoy myself. Although money is important I hope that it wouldn't influence my decision to do something. I would very much like to work with my hands especially in the field of woodwork. I enjoy working with tools already and I also enjoy making things from wood.
   When I was on holiday my parents visited a craftsman who had started his own small company – it had about two or three other people in it. He was making beautiful modern furniture out of unusual woods. He would even make things to what the customer wanted. My parents wanted a special shelf unit, for example, and together with my father he drew what they wanted. A few months later the shelf unit was completed.
   This is the type of work I would also like to do. It is interesting, varied and brings me into contact with people. It's also work that is to do with one's hands and being creative at the same time. This is what is important to me. (…)

Group discussion

1. need for education / Maths, German, English are important / could do more / need for computer knowledge / need for independence / need to know how to do or look for things / basic skills / social integration / your experiences / your opinions / …

2. hard / few jobs / need to be mobile / flexible / unemployment situation in Germany and your area / hope for jobs / need for experience / make oneself interesting / believe in oneself / any job vacancy can be mine as much as anyone else's / attitudes / importance of school work / your experiences / your opinions / …

3. qualities / skills / exam results / the person – appearance, personality, interesting, reliable, honest, willing to learn … / ask for: introductions, about themselves, their interest in the job and their skills, opinions about working late and private life, reaction to criticism, their hobbies, sport, outside interests / …

Sicher durch alle Klassen!

Faktenwissen und praxisgerechte Übungen mit vollständigen Lösungen.

Mathematik

Mathematik 5. Klasse Bayern ... Best.-Nr. 91410
Mathematik 8. Klasse Bayern ... Best.-Nr. 91406
Funktionen 8.–10. Klasse Bayern ... Best.-Nr. 91408
Lineare Gleichungssysteme ... Best.-Nr. 900122
Bruchzahlen und Dezimalbrüche ... Best.-Nr. 900061
Formelsammlung Mathematik
Realschule 7.–10. Klasse Hessen ... Best.-Nr. 61411
Kompakt-Wissen Algebra ... Best.-Nr. 90016
Kompakt-Wissen Geometrie ... Best.-Nr. 90026
Entwicklung mathematischer Fähigkeiten
ab 4. Klasse, Teil 1: Algebra ... Best.-Nr. 990403
Entwicklung mathematischer Fähigkeiten
ab 4. Klasse, Teil 2: Geometrie ... Best.-Nr. 990405
Übertritt in weiterführende Schulen
4. Klasse ... Best.-Nr. 990404
Übertritt in weiterführende Schulen ... Best.-Nr. 90002

Orientierungsarbeit Mathematik Realschulabschluss Sachsen

Orientierungsarbeit Mathematik
Klassenstufe 8
Realschulbildungsgang Sachsen ... Best.-Nr. 1415081

Betriebswirtschaftslehre/ Rechnungswesen

Training 9. Klasse Bayern ... Best.-Nr. 91471
Training 9. Klasse Bayern – Lösungen ... Best.-Nr. 91471L
Training 10. Klasse Bayern ... Best.-Nr. 91472
Training 10. Klasse Bayern – Lösungen ... Best.-Nr. 91472L

Deutsch

Rechtschreibung und Diktat
5./6. Klasse ... Best.-Nr. 90408
Grammatik und Stil 5./6. Klasse ... Best.-Nr. 50406
Aufsatz 5./6. Klasse ... Best.-Nr. 90401
Grammatik und Stil 7./8. Klasse ... Best.-Nr. 90407
Aufsatz 7./8. Klasse ... Best.-Nr. 91442
Aufsatz 9./10. Klasse
Realschule Baden-Württemberg ... Best.-Nr. 81440
Deutsch 9./10. Klasse Journalistische Texte lesen,
auswerten, schreiben ... Best.-Nr. 81442
Deutsche Rechtschreibung 5.–10. Klasse ... Best.-Nr. 90402
Text-Kompendien zum Kompetenzbereich
„Verstehen und Nutzen von Texten"
Band 1: „Der olympische Gedanke –
und die Welt des Sports" ... Best.-Nr. 81443
Band 2: „Demokratie leben heißt sich
verantwortlich fühlen und sich einmischen" ... Best.-Nr. 81444
Kompakt-Wissen Rechtschreibung ... Best.-Nr. 944065
Lexikon zur Kinder- und Jugendliteratur ... Best.-Nr. 93443

Englisch

Englisch Grundwissen 5. Klasse ... Best.-Nr. 50505
Englisch – Hörverstehen 5. Klasse mit CD ... Best.-Nr. 90512
Englisch – Rechtschreibung und Diktat
5. Klasse mit 3 CDs ... Best.-Nr. 90531
Englisch – Leseverstehen 5. Klasse ... Best.-Nr. 90526
Englisch – Wortschatzübung 5. Klasse mit CD .. Best.-Nr. 90518
Englisch Grundwissen 6. Klasse ... Best.-Nr. 90506
Englisch – Hörverstehen 6. Klasse mit CD ... Best.-Nr. 90511
Englisch – Rechtschreibung und Diktat
6. Klasse mit CD ... Best.-Nr. 90532
Englisch – Leseverstehen 6. Klasse ... Best.-Nr. 90525
Englisch – Wortschatzübung 6. Klasse mit CD Best.-Nr. 90519
Englisch Grundwissen 7. Klasse ... Best.-Nr. 90507
Englisch – Hörverstehen 7. Klasse mit CD ... Best.-Nr. 90513
Englisch Grundwissen 8. Klasse ... Best.-Nr. 90508
Englisch – Leseverstehen 8. Klasse ... Best.-Nr. 90522
Comprehension 1 / 8. Klasse ... Best.-Nr. 91453
Englisch Grundwissen 9. Klasse ... Best.-Nr. 90509
Englisch – Hörverstehen 9. Klasse mit CD ... Best.-Nr. 90515
Englische Rechtschreibung 9./10. Klasse ... Best.-Nr. 80453
Translation Practice 1 / ab 9. Klasse ... Best.-Nr. 80451
Comprehension 2 / 9. Klasse ... Best.-Nr. 91452
Textproduktion 9./10. Klasse ... Best.-Nr. 90541
Englisch Grundwissen 10. Klasse ... Best.-Nr. 90510
Englisch – Hörverstehen 10. Klasse mit CD ... Best.-Nr. 91457
Englisch – Leseverstehen 10. Klasse ... Best.-Nr. 90521
Translation Practice 2 / ab 10. Klasse ... Best.-Nr. 80452
Comprehension 3 / 10. Klasse ... Best.-Nr. 91454
Systematische Vokabelsammlung ... Best.-Nr. 91455

Französisch

Französisch – Sprechsituationen und
Dolmetschen mit 2 CDs ... Best.-Nr. 91461
Rechtschreibung und Diktat
1./2. Lernjahr mit 2 CDs ... Best.-Nr. 905501
Französisch – Wortschatzübung Mittelstufe ... Best.-Nr. 94510

Ratgeber für Schüler

Richtig Lernen
Tipps und Lernstrategien – Unterstufe ... Best.-Nr. 10481
Richtig Lernen
Tipps und Lernstrategien – Mittelstufe ... Best.-Nr. 10482

(Bitte blättern Sie um)